CONTENTS

ABOUT THE AUTHOR

Dr. Almeida is an Assistant Professor of Communications Media at Indiana University of Pennsylvania. He is also a Keynote Speaker who has published over a dozen academic articles in the field of Communication. Dr. Almeida is also the author of other writing books e.g., *Writing the Phenomenological Qualitative Dissertation Step-by-Step*. He lives in Indiana, PA, with his wife and family.

ACKNOWLEDGEMENTS

First and foremost, I acknowledge the immense role that Dr. Kurt Dudt has played in this book with his guidance, help, and willingness to share. I also acknowledge the role that my advisor, Dr. Alison Carr-Chellman, has played in my career in the field of Communications. I am forever grateful for the lessons I learned from them both.

I also thank my wife Amanda for her support, as well as my parents for always being "there" for me when I needed them the most. God is my witness that I love them all.

Finally, I acknowledge several students who have helped me in a number of ways with this book: Chris Mason, Kyra Barron, Matthew McClelland, Jamie Root, Suzie Ranish, Jamie Owoc, Quinn Denio, and Alyssa St. Clair.

I am grateful for them all. Thank you.

Luis C. Almeida, Ph.D.

Scriptwriting
Step-by-Step

Pearson Learning Solutions, 501 Boylston Street, Suite 900,
Boston, MA 02116
A Pearson Education Company
www.pearsoned.com

Printed in the United States of America

1 2 3 4 5 6 7 8 9 10 V0CR 17 16 15 14 13 12

000200010271712181

TS

ISBN 10: 1-256-87137-0
ISBN 13: 978-1-256-87137-8

1

SCRIPTWRITING

"If it's a good script I'll do it. And if it's a bad script, and they pay me enough, I'll do it." George Burns

LEARNING OBJECTIVES

By the end of the chapter, learners will be able to:

1. Name three strategies for writing great scripts.
2. Explain why certain words are not good to be used in scriptwriting.
3. Identify strategies for writing great scripts.

INTRODUCTION

Writing can be quite intense, especially if you haven't practiced. There are, however, different kinds of writing (Garvey & Rivers, 1982). You can write for newspapers, for magazines, and in this day and age, for the web. Writing scripts is different than writing for newspapers or journalistic writing. In this chapter, I will explain to you how to become an AVID scriptwriter, without making things complicated. I will simplify the steps you will have to take in order to produce what I call "rapid scripts."

BEFORE WE START . . .

Before I start talking about the actual criteria for writing scripts, I probably should put things in perspective for you. Scriptwriting is a skill, much like golf. When I was a teenager, I played a lot of golf. In fact, I was able, after working on my golf skills, to play for the Junior Brazilian National Golf Team. I can assure you that playing a sport for any country isn't an activity that occurs overnight. Most people don't realize the amount of time and effort that is required to master a skill and compete at the national and international level. Scriptwriting isn't different in this regard. In order for you to produce scripts, you will need to understand that your skills in scriptwriting will evolve and will get better over time, if you practice.

One of the biggest mistakes I have seen when it comes to scriptwriting is the assumption that if you write for one medium it will automatically transfer to another. Although it helps to understand how to write for the web, writing scripts for radio is really different than writing for the web or for television. Understanding these basic premises and mindsets can help you to become a better scriptwriter.

LET'S GET OUR HANDS WET

Scriptwriting is about writing and writing well under a specific format. Different formats will call for different styles of writing and formats. You must check your spelling (Garvey & Rivers, 1982) because without it, speakers will have a tough time reading on the air. In my third year as a faculty member, I helped a colleague by becoming a DJ in our college's radio station. I can assure you that spelling words correctly was a necessity at the Dr. A show. My reputation was on the line, as well as the reputation of our radio station and university. If you want to produce great scripts, you must know how to spell correctly. I can also assure you that stations have a low tolerance policy—some even have a zero tolerance policy—towards script errors, which could either result in a media professional to lose their job (Garvey & Rivers, 1982) or a station to reject the script.

THINGS TO AVOID

In scriptwriting, we have what I call the "no-no" list. These are things you MUST avoid at all costs. For your benefit, I decided to include the "no-no" list up front so that you understand that these things are simply unacceptable. So let's get started.

- **Redundancy.** As a competent scriptwriter, you are to avoid redundancy at all costs. Please do not use the same phrase over and over again. It makes your script less creative, repetitive, and can misguide the reader. Although you might want to say the phone number more than once (on some occasions), having the same phrase in different parts of the script can be problematic.
- **Foul language and jargon.** A professional scriptwriter cannot use inadequate language, especially foul language and jargon. Your job is to write clean and legible, without words and phrases that the audience can't understand and/or are offensive to the public.
- **Lack of clarity.** If your writing isn't clear, you won't become an effective scriptwriter. **<u>DO NOT</u>** repeat the same words over and over. In reality, this is a bit tricky because some degree of repetition is fine, such as in commercials where important words must be repeated at least three times.
- **Writing too extensively.** Don't make scriptwriting extensive. Your job is to write well and concisely because each word has a price. If you can tell the story in ten words, why use thirty-five? Scriptwriting is a skill that must be mastered and it must be written to the point.
- **Avoid long sentences.** Make sure that your script has only one single idea (Garvey & Rivers, 1982). Presenting multiple ideas simultaneously can cause information overload and make the script ineffective resulting in listeners to either lose track of what the message is about or simply ignore your script.
- **Avoid difficult words.** There is a correlation between having difficult words and error. To put it simply, difficult words increase the chance of an error. If your script has difficult

words, listeners might not be able to decode the meaning of the message or might not know what the words mean. If they don't know what the words mean, they can't understand what you want them to understand.

- **Clichés and buzzwords.** Don't use clichés or buzzwords because the listener may not know what they mean over time or may not want to listen to them. What is popular today might not be popular tomorrow or next month. What was popular in the '70s is not as popular today, is it? Buzzwords come and go (Garvey & Rivers, 1982) but a cliché stays.

SAMPLE OF CLICHÉS

There are tons of clichés in American English. Have you heard the phrase, "You are a jack of all trades!" or "I don't give a damn" or even the old one, "Give me a break." Clichés are to be avoided at all costs. The list below is just a small example of what is out there. This list can be quite substantial and it increases day by day.

could care less	snug as a bug	still waters run deep
out of pocket	off the wagon	kick ass
but seriously	behind the eight ball	read my lips
bottom line	experts agree	tough as nails
easy as pie	born yesterday	death's doorstep
give a damn	wheeler-dealer	wolf at the door
count your blessings	no guts, no glory	jump the gun
worst nightmare	few and far between	neat as a pin

SAMPLE BUZZWORDS

Buzzwords are as much of a "no-no" as clichés. A buzzword is a word without any significance, but folks believe it has meaning. Words like America, Chimerica, and cash for clunkers are samples of them. There is no room for buzzwords in professional scriptwriting.

Chimerica	snug as a bug	still waters run deep
out of pocket	off the wagon	kick ass
but seriously	behind the eight ball	read my lips
bottom line	experts agree	tough as nails
easy as pie	born yesterday	death's doorstep
give a damn	wheeler-dealer	wolf at the door
count your blessings	no guts, no glory	jump the gun
worst nightmare	few and far between	neat as a pin

OTHER THINGS TO AVOID

- **Large numbers of objectives.** This is particularly problematic if you are developing scripts for audio. It makes scriptwriting too rich for the media. A professional scriptwriter should use only enough objectives to get the point across. Having a large number of objectives can make your job more complicated. Would you like to complicate your work?
- **Don't use passive verbs.** There is no time for passive verbs in scriptwriting. It will make your script too expensive and dull. Avoid the passive voice! In addition to being dull and expensive, passive voice is almost always seen as boring and too long to listen to, which can result in listener's withdrawal. My recommendation is that you avoid this at all costs.
- **Avoid too much detail.** Different from print and web media where detail is acceptable, scriptwriting especially for broadcast is to be avoided. Your job is to produce a script that producers can use, maybe refine. Although scriptwriting is about writing, it isn't about "overwriting." Detail can be fine; however, too much detail is a "no-no."

THINGS TO DO

In this section, I will explain to you what you should do in order to write great scripts. What I am going to propose is not complicated and it isn't supposed to be. It is, in fact, a to-the-point list for you to get your scripts done effectively and efficiently. Remember, in the scriptwriting world, those who win the prize are the ones who can write great scripts more efficiently. For this reason, I will tell you precisely which rules to follow. They are listed below.

- **Know your audience.** You are to understand who you are talking to. This section is so important that I dedicated a full chapter in this book to talk about it. In brief, you should know who will be listening to your scripts.
- **Use the words you know well.** It is much easier to write well if you know the words well. The secret to knowing words is to read well. If you read well, you write well. When was the last time you read a book? Remember, your scripts will get better as you read this book! Why? Because you are reading. If you read and build your vocabulary, you should write better over time.
- **Start sentences with a powerful statement.** YES! Why do you need to wait to make a splash? I am not aware of too many listeners who enjoy waiting 30+ seconds to discover what the script is about. Make it known quickly with powerful words. If you do this, you can't go wrong.
- **Write in a conversational style.** Am I not writing as I am talking with you? Don't you understand what I am saying? More often than not, people understand the meaning of your scripts by how conversational your tone is. It is human nature to have a conversation, isn't it? Why not capitalize on a technique you already do as a person?
- **Write with simplicity.** When I was a kid, I remember reading a Brazilian proverb that went like this, "I want to live a simple life, so that I could grow up simple, graduate from high school simple, college simple, have kids simple, work simple to one day—retire famous, rich and simple." Let's apply this to scriptwriting. The proverb would be, "I want to live a life where I write scripts simple, so that I could grow up writing simple scripts, graduate from college, have kids, and work with scriptwriting simple to one day—retire famous, rich and writing SIMPLE scripts."

QUICK REVIEW

- ✓ Scriptwriting is about writing and writing well under a specific format
- ✓ Avoid redundancy
- ✓ Avoid foul language and jargon
- ✓ Avoid lack of clarity
- ✓ Avoid writing too extensively
- ✓ Avoid long sentences
- ✓ Avoid difficult words
- ✓ Avoid clichés and buzzwords
- ✓ Avoid large numbers of objectives
- ✓ Avoid passive verbs
- ✓ Avoid too much detail
- ✓ You are to know your audience
- ✓ You are to use the words you know well
- ✓ You are to start sentences with a powerful statement
- ✓ You are to write in a conversational style
- ✓ You are to write with simplicity

QUESTIONS

1. Name three strategies for writing great scripts.
2. Why aren't certain words good to use in scriptwriting?
3. What happens if you use difficult words?
4. Should you provide a lot of detail? Defend your position.

SAMPLE EXERCISE (Mason)

Standing approximately 5′ 10″, Mr. Harris enters the room. Charlie Harris is a well-known friend of mine, and there aren't too many people like him. He is a unique individual who I have had the pleasure of knowing for about a year and a half. He has the appearance and skin tone of a Native American but is not tied to them by race. He is a Caucasian male whose lineage goes back to Ireland.

His short buzzed hair is very dark brown and it sits on top of his very round head. Looking at Charlie you know that he is a nice guy, and most of the time he is wearing clothing from outdoor brands. He truly is a woodsman. His eyes are usually half open but he is in good healthy shape and weighs about 175 pounds. It is not uncommon for him to always be wearing boots and having a honeyberry backwoods cigar hanging out of the side of his mouth. He always has a five o'clock shadow and sometimes he gets red cheeks when it is cold outside.

Charlie is a man of bold actions and precision. His precision can become sloppy at times but the job gets done no matter what. Being physical is something that Charlie is very in tune with. Building things with his hands and keeping busy are traits that describe what he does on a day-to-day basis. He is NEVER afraid to take action. He is the first on the scene and he gets this from his extensive training at the local fire department and from his rigorous experience with a quick response team, which is very similar to an EMS team. Like I have said before, it is not uncommon for Charlie to be smiling and laughing about 90% of the day. He is also very genuine and has a strong sense of manners, which is attributed to his upbringing.

Charlie is a simple guy, but genuine, and a friend that will never let you down. He is constantly thinking about how he can help people in any way possible. His favorite thing in the world is to be in the woods and among nature. He calls the woods home and would live in the middle of the woods for the rest of his life at any given time. He is very "manly" and is very American. He has a strong sense of nationalism, which comes from his father and from his service as a volunteer fireman. Some also comes from his family because his father is a guard at the jail. Growing up with a father that deals with inmates would have an effect on how you think because you have to be tough so the prisoners could not get to you. This is a trait that he gets from his father. He is serious but is always looking for fun. He is a happy-go-lucky kind of guy but doesn't take lip from anyone and will crack you if you are being mean to him or his friends. He won't think twice about it and will usually ask questions after people are knocked out. He will defend you and stick by your side no matter what so you would always want him on your side.

Charlie has a unique chuckle that is very particular and very often heard. He is always laughing and smiling. Being brought up in the Pittsburgh area he has an unmistakable Pittsburgh accent. From *"Yinz"* to *"Crick"* these are all words that are a part of his vocabulary. His tone is about mid-range but when he is excited about something he can get very loud and is always laughing. When he is angry that is another story; he can mouth off and cuss whenever he feels like.

At first Charlie is shy but if you are well acquainted with him, he does not have an edit button. He enjoys spending as much time as he can with his friends and girlfriend. His girlfriend is important in his life and she keeps him on track because he has a short attention span. He likes hanging out in a social setting and even interacts like this when homework is on the chopping block.

EXERCISE

You are to do a characterization on a person that you know well. In about two pages, with a 12 point Times font, 1 inch margin, and 1.5 space, describe to me this person, with five components of characterization. I will be looking for the quality of your detailed work. Don't write, "I know Kristen. She is cool and nice." Rather, you could write, "Kristen is my best friend. She is tall, nice, with blond hair and full of enthusiasm. . . ." Create a bullet list of traits about the person you know.

2

AUDIENCE ANALYSIS

"God is a comedian, playing to an audience too afraid to laugh."
Voltaire

LEARNING OBJECTIVES

By the end of the chapter, learners will be able to:

1. Name two reasons you understand your circumstances when analyzing your audience.
2. Know what will happen if your script isn't good enough.
3. List two types of audience analyses and three techniques.
4. Name three demographic subcategories.
5. Name three psychographic subcategories.

INTRODUCTION

One of a scriptwriter's main goals is to analyze the audience. I would go further to state that the secret of successful scriptwriters is knowing their audience. Who are they? Where do they come from? Are they male or female? Are they from the USA or abroad? Are they in their 20s? 30s? 40s? These questions and more must be answered prior to writing any script for the media. Writing a script and failing to tailor it to your audience is one of the single worse mistakes you can make. You are to write your script with your audience in mind. You are to think, "What will my audience think about my script?" If they (the audience) don't feel they are being addressed, they will not listen to your script. Don't forget, you have a sophisticated and demanding audience. One of the best approaches to keep them tuned in is to understand who they are.

THE REALITY OF YOUR CIRCUMSTANCES

The audience will, more often than not, think of themselves as experts! In the age of social networking and interactivity, the audience now thinks they are experts in film, radio, web, TV, and in writing scripts because they now can write "scripts." This could be a major challenge depending on the assignment you were given. Don't forget—in the 21st century, the untrained audience believes they are TV critics because they can provide feedback on the station's website or on YouTube. They will also judge and criticize your script if they have a chance. Be aware of your circumstances and react accordingly. You are to understand your environment. Perhaps the future will change and we will work as professionals did in the past. I am, however, skeptical. Just don't forget the *Almeida Motto* scriptwriting statement: "Your audience is expecting the highest quality script you can produce. Don't forget that."

WHAT HAPPENS IF YOUR SCRIPT "SUCKS"

You will be in trouble if your script sucks. You might want to start a campaign to look for another career. You **CANNOT** afford to produce scripts that suck. Trust me. Your audience will not pay attention, not only to your script but also to you. Your audience won't watch your show and will probably resent your work. Once you make a noticeable mistake, you will lose your audience and your reputation as a scriptwriter is ruined. I don't know of any other way of conveying this to you but to tell you the way it is. If I was looking for an entry-level career as a scriptwriter, I would take this advice seriously. If you want to make a mark in the media field, chances are you will need to understand scriptwriting pretty well. My advice? Master it, have fun with it, and **DON'T** suck.

WHAT DO YOU THINK YOUR GOAL IS?

Your goal, when it comes to scriptwriting, is to eventually intrigue your audience and make your audience feel important. You are to ensure that they remember that you made them feel that way! In order to do this, you will need to know quite a lot about who you are trying to reach, e.g., audience's age, type of upbringing, economic status, if they are sustainers, achievers, integrators, or society conscious. More importantly, you will need to convey a message to them in a way they understand. Therefore, your goal is to analyze and write scripts for them so they understand. Your job starts with what to look for in an audience: demographics.

WHAT TO LOOK FOR IN AN AUDIENCE (Demographics)

It starts with understanding demographics. Demographics can be understood as the overall characteristics of a population. It is as simple as that. Characteristics of populations include gender, level of economic status, education status, race, and ethnicity, to name a few. Within each category, there are subcategories. For example, in gender, we have males and females. When it comes to income, we could have low, medium, or high income. We could also operationalize income numerically, e.g., <10K, 20K–50K, 60K–100K, and >100K. This, of course, is just classification. What really matters is that you understand that demographics is an important variable in writing scripts and that the criterion associated with your classifications is as important. Other demographics include whether the population is part of the baby boomers or millenniums, or whether they are techie or traditional. Make sure you understand the demographics of your audience!

WHAT TO LOOK FOR IN AN AUDIENCE (Psychographics)

In addition to demographics, the scriptwriter must also work on psychographics. Psychographics can be understood as analyses that break down a particular population by its lifestyle characteristics. Value, attitudes, and lifestyles (VALS), is a framework developed by

Arnold Mitchell and his colleagues in 1978 and serves as the basis for psychographics in this book. They came up with a number of lifestyle types including integrators, sustainers, achievers, society conscious, experimentals, survivors, belongers, I-Am-Me, and emulators.

- **Integrators.** These individuals are creative and prosperous and often experiment with market products and innovative ways to solve problems. They have stamina and are the ones doing what has to be done in order to achieve what they want.
- **Sustainers.** These individuals are people who live paycheck to paycheck. They are often hopeless to improve their lifestyle and are rarely looking for extravagance.
- **Achievers.** These individuals are decision makers and prosperous people toward whom advertisement is often directed. They are not TV watchers, though. This population tends to look for information creatively.
- **Society conscious.** This group is aware of social developments and problems with society and is often politically proactive and vocal. They often read a lot and are informed and use their knowledge to serve society.
- **Experimentals.** They are a bold population and are often trying new things for the heck of it. They tend to consist of an upscale audience who enjoy adrenaline rushes.
- **Survivors.** These are the folks who are barely making it. They are on the fringe of making or breaking. They are often without money and do what they can to make it.
- **Belongers.** This group conforms and are satisfied with the flow. They have safe values and dislike change. They would be considered laggards in innovation diffusion. They are not bold, often watch TV, and belong to the middle class.
- **I-Am-Me.** They are people who live to make themselves look different, and even may be members of a subculture. More often than not, rebellious youth are part of this VALS category.
- **Emulators.** This group can be characterized as wanting a better life but lacking the knowledge to be able to move up the ladder of society. They are often looking for status and a path to a good life.

TYPES OF ANALYSES AND TECHNIQUES

There are different types of audience analyses and techniques. I could write a complete book about this topic alone, but for the purposes of this book let's narrow the analyses to cohort and geo-demographics. With that said, let's rock and roll.

- **Cohort analysis.** One of the best ways to understand cohort analysis is by tying it to demographics. I would argue that cohort analysis is a specialized form of demographics used to identify generations and then design and produce products with generational appeal. Your goal is to investigate what makes one be a part of the X generation? What are some of the characteristics of a postwar generation? Can we assume that a depression survivor is going to behave in a particular way? How about a hippie from the '60s?

Examples of cohort analyses include depression survivors who came of age during the economic depression of the '30s; World War II veterans who came of age in the '40s; postwar generations who came of age in the 1950's; baby boomers, who came of age in the late '60s and '70s; Generation Xers, who came of age in 1980; and millenniums who came of age in the '90s.

- **Geo-demographics.** This is a contemporary method of audience analysis that provides lifestyle breakdowns. The categories are: blue-chip blues—these are the wealthiest blue-collar suburbs; young suburbia—also known as childbearing outlying suburbs; golden ponds—rustic mountains or seashore or lakeside cottage communities; blue-blood states—these are the wealthiest neighborhoods; money and brains—they can be categorized as big city enclaves of townhouses, condos, and apartments.

In order to generate these analyses, you will need some techniques. One of the most obvious is online investigation. With the advent of the internet, information is now available at your fingertips. A competent scriptwriter wanting to conduct an audience analysis should probably spend time investigating information online.

Another technique you should use is going to the library and investigating print material. This also includes the periodicals and microfilm sections. These are rich sources of reliable information. You should also be ready to interview the population you want to write scripts for. Be advised! Prior to interviewing anybody, you might need their permission through a consent form and/or an interview protocol.

QUICK REVIEW

- ✓ The audience will, more often than not, think of themselves as experts. You are to understand your environment.
- ✓ If your script is not good enough, your audience will not pay attention to you or your script.
- ✓ Demographics can be understood as the overall characteristics of a population. It is as simple as that. Characteristics of populations include their gender, level of economic status, education status, race, and ethnicity, to name a few.
- ✓ Demographics and psychographics are two types of audience analyses.
- ✓ Integrators, sustainers, and achievers are three types of psychographic subcategories.
- ✓ Gender, social economic status, and level of education are examples of demographical data.
- ✓ Money and brains, blue-blood states, and golden ponds are examples of geo-demographics.

QUESTIONS

1. Why should you capture demographic and psychographic data?
2. List and explain two types of psychographic subcategories.
3. If you were hired as an entry-level scriptwriter, what would you do?
4. Explain cohort analysis.
5. When is it appropriate to produce a bad script?

SAMPLE EXERCISE (MASON)

Audience Background

Collecting information on an audience's background is essential to writing a good script. The audience that we are analyzing is going to have at least a high school diploma. The type of audience that we are going to analyze is going to be similar to an outdoor channel. We are analyzing them because many of them are blue-collar workers and will relate to the outdoors and enjoy being in nature. The audience has a middle class socio-economic status and provide for their families by harvesting from the outdoors. The demographic that generally watches outdoor shows is of Caucasian. Their reference of technology in this field of script would relate to how scientifically advanced hunting products and technology are in relation to the outdoors. Hunters are always looking to improve their chances with harvesting an animal and will take any edge they can get.

The population of the audience is generally from rural areas or small towns. This demographic is very interesting because a small percentage of them are very financially stable and among the top shelf of corporate America. The income level is usually 20k and above. This demographic has a very strong respect for the outdoors and wants to protect it at all costs.

Psychographic Subcategories

The psychographics of the audience is categorized as sustainer and experimental. The sustainer part of the population is trying to protect the outdoors and a great deal of their money goes for what they like doing: hunting. We also can look at the audience's thrill and adrenaline rush they get from the hunt. If we are looking to impose advertising toward them we are going to play off of this at all costs. The experimental psychographics are always looking for their next rush, and when a new technology comes out they are the first to purchase it as long as they can still provide for themselves (sustainers).

Major Categorization

The categorization of the audience is going to fall between the baby boomers and Generation X. The audience is strongly weighted in the baby boomers category because they have passed the tradition on to future generations. This is very interesting because each generation has the power to either pass on the tradition or let it slip away. Slowly the numbers of the audience decrease over generations, but the popularity of hunting shows and programs that involve the outdoors has had a few rebirths over the years, and out of all the programs involves more technology than many fields of interest.

EXERCISE

You are to conduct an audience analysis for a script you want to produce. Make sure that you address only **ONE** audience. You **MUST** include the following components in your final document:

- **Audience background.** You are to list their gender, age range, levels of education, social-economic status, ethnicity, and technology background.
- **Psychographic subcategories.** You are to also include which psychographic subcategory you are going to address and why.
- **Major categorization.** Make sure your audience analysis has a clear and objective generalization about the population you want to reach, e.g., Generation Xers or millenniums and their characteristics. You will need to do some investigation here.

3

COPYRIGHT

"Certainly the interest in asserting copyright is a justified one."
Johannes Rau

LEARNING OBJECTIVES

By the end of the chapter, learners will be able to:

1. Explain why violating copyright laws is a bad idea.
2. Summarize copyright laws when it comes to scriptwriting.
3. Name reasons why contemporary youth might have problems with copyright laws.
4. List three types of copyright works.

INTRODUCTION

Scripts are copyrightable. Because of this simple fact alone, we should talk about copyright. We won't however, spend too much time talking about the detailed intricacies of copyright laws, as this isn't a class in law school. We will, however, address questions of copyright as they apply to scriptwriting. Basically, copyrights protect the "original works of authorship" that are fixed in a tangible form of expression. In colloquial terms, copyright protects you from anybody wanting to steal your work. Would you like to have someone steal your scripts to produce a movie in Hollywood and make millions without giving you any form of compensation? I would be upset, wouldn't you? Failing to understand copyright can be a big problem for the scriptwriter both in terms of his own work or the work of others.

HOW DO YOU COPYRIGHT YOUR WORK?

You can copyright your scripts by sending a copy of your work, in tangible format, to the U.S. Copyright Office. It is important to understand that your work is copyrighted the moment you create and put it into a tangible format. However, if you need to go to court due to copyright infringement, you will need to have your work registered at the copyright office. Also, having your works registered with the U.S. Copyright Office will put your works on public record and you, in return, will receive a certificate of registration. I have to tell you. It feels pretty good to have certificates of registration available to you, on paper. I have a few of those and it makes me happy just to see them in my files.

PRESENT DAY COPYRIGHT CHALLENGES

Copyright's mission today is the same as it was 100 years ago. Its main mission is to protect the "original works of authorship" of a person. What has changed substantially are people's beliefs of what is copyrighted and what isn't. It is common for college students to go online and get photographs and scripts for their own use, without giving proper credit to the sources. In our present days, folks post copyrighted motion pictures on YouTube and Vimeo, thinking it is OKAY because they are not making a profit from it. YouTube and Vimeo one day will either diminish in importance and/or cease to exist. However, copyright laws and infringement of copyrighted materials are not going anywhere anytime soon. One of the major challenges I face as a professor, when it comes to copyrighted materials, is to tell the student that it isn't okay to download music from peer-to-peer networks and that videos and images are owned by somebody, even though they might be available online. It is tough to talk with students about it these days because a large number of people are doing it and sometimes, they just "don't believe" OR don't want to believe and be accountable. For example, in one of my classes, several students asked the question "Why can't I get that YouTube video and use it in my project willingly?" or "You know, it wasn't me who took the CNN video out and put it onto YouTube." My response was the following, "The video wasn't created by XYZ YouTube account. It was produced by CNN professionals!" Technically, I could have said that he (the student) could use 30 seconds of that clip, due to fair use laws, but the lesson had to be given—AND, I "knew" he would probably use more than 30 seconds anyway.

Scriptwriters have to be very careful to NOT go online and download the work of others. It isn't worth it and agencies investigate. The challenges are obvious. The millenniums were raised in an era of double standards without fully understanding the implications of violation of copyright laws. Just because scripts might be available online does not mean that they may be used freely. Scriptwriting is about writing! A lot of writing! Your OWN writing.

TYPES OF COPYRIGHT WORKS

There are a large number of works that can be copyrightable, beyond what it is referred to as "poor man's copyright," or simply going to the post office, sending your own work to yourself, and claiming copyright. The items below are just a few examples of works that can be copyrighted.

- Literary works
- Musical works
- Dramatic works
- Pantomimes and choreographic works
- Motion picture and other audio/visual works
- Sound recordings
- Architectural works

Scriptwriting falls under literary works. These items are copyrightable: poems, novels, articles, newspaper articles, and scripts. So, be aware that your work is protected by law and that the work of others is also protected by law. Understanding this simple process can save your career in the field.

IT IS AS SIMPLE AS THIS

Look, this is what you need to know about copyrights when it comes to scriptwriting. Scripts are protected; you must not copy the works of others and claim it as your own. You can protect your works by simply producing it and putting it in a tangible format, but if you want to take somebody to court, you will need your work copyrighted at the U.S. Copyright Office. Just because "things" are available online doesn't mean that you can use them at your own will. Somebody owns the content and if you want to use it, you will need to ask permission to do so. Copyright protection is the same today as it was in 1850! You are to respect the works of others.

QUICK REVIEW

- ✓ Scripts are copyrightable. Basically, copyrights protect the "original works of authorship" that are fixed in a tangible form of expression.
- ✓ You can copyright your scripts by sending a copy of your work, in tangible format, to the U.S. Copyright Office.
- ✓ Copyright's mission today is the same as 100 years ago. It's main mission is to protect the "original works of authorship" of a person.
- ✓ Scriptwriters have to be very careful to NOT go online and download the work of others.
- ✓ There are a large number of works that can be copyrightable, beyond what it is referred to as "poor man's copyright" or simply going to the post office, sending your own work to yourself, and claiming copyright.
- ✓ Scriptwriting falls under literary works. These items are copyrightable: poems, novels, articles, newspaper articles, and scripts.

✓ You can protect your works by simply producing them and putting them in a tangible format but if you want to take somebody to court, you will need your work copyrighted at the U.S. Copyright Office.

QUESTIONS

1. What would happen if you gather scripts online without permission?
2. Is a work automatically copyrighted?
3. Scriptwriting falls under which kind of copyrighted work?
4. What do you mean by "original works of authorship"?
5. Explain poor man's copyright.

SAMPLE EXERCISE (McClelland, Root, Ranish)

Before submitting a script, we would first analyze who our target audience would be. Once we establish which demographics and psychographics that we are choosing, we would begin to write a script. We must be careful not to use any ideas or information that have already been used and copyrighted, in order to avoid plagiarism and pirating information.

Finding data and ideas online could lead to unintentional plagiarism. We believe that it is unethical to go online and steal someone else's ideas and writing, however using ideas to brainstorm our own new project would be an acceptable process. Under these circumstances, we would not copyright our work and put it into a tangible form because that would be considered stealing someone's work, which is illegal.

If we went online and stole the plot or script from *Friends*, and put it online as our own work, everyone would be able to recognize that we had plagiarized. Because the writers for *Friends* had their scripts copyrighted, they are entitled to take necessary legal actions against us. By not putting it into a tangible form, we would not be plagiarizing because we would not be trying to pass off someone else's work as our own work.

In order to avoid these problems, we would come up with original ideas and scripts. We would avoid gathering data and information online and using it directly in our script. We would make sure not to cut any corners and be aware of all the copyright laws. Citing sources and information could help elude any copyright infringement lawsuits while giving credit where credit is deserved. We would then have our work copyrighted. There are two ways we could do this: we could either mail our work to ourselves which is known as the "poor man's copyright." Or, we could send a copy of our work to the U.S. Copyright Office. This would protect our work from being plagiarized in other concepts.

EXERCISE

In a group of 5 students, you are to discuss the following: "You are a professional scriptwriter who wants to produce a script for a movie in Hollywood. You investigate the protocols and procedures required for you to complete your goal and decide to cut some corners. You go online, gather some data, put together a rough draft of the script, put it into a tangible format, and put it online in his/her blog for feedback. In this exercise, you are to:

- Talk about the implications of the plan above.
- Would you consider the protocol an ethical one, yes/no? Why? Give examples.
- Would you have produced a script and put into a tangible format, under the circumstances?
- What would you have done differently, in order to make this process more professional?

4

CAMERA SHOTS, ANGLES, AND MOVEMENTS

"A style is not a matter of camera angles or fancy footwork, it's an expression, an accurate expression of your particular opinion."
Karel Reisz

LEARNING OBJECTIVES

By the end of the chapter, learners will be able to:

1. Name five different camera shots.
2. Differentiate between wide angles and close-up angles.
3. Explain what OSS means.
4. List three types of angle shots.
5. List three types of camera movements.

INTRODUCTION

Understanding camera shots, angles, and movement is a necessity for novice scriptwriters as you will need to understand how to use them in your scripts. Failing to understand this simple and straightforward tenet can be the difference between those who have their scripts accepted for production and those who complain that the field is unjust, or simply not good to be in. Don't be like them, pay <u>VERY</u>

<u>CLOSE ATTENTION</u> to this chapter. The scriptwriter must be able to talk and write like a scriptwriter in the same way that a physician must talk and write as a physician.

PRELIMINARY DISCUSSIONS ON CAMERA

We could talk about the different types of cameras, e.g., SLR and point to shoot cameras, aperture, f-stops and all that cool stuff. However, we won't because this book is about scriptwriting not photography. For the photography discussion, I would recommend that you read Scott Kelby's books on digital photography.

Understanding the different types of camera shots, angles, and movements is paramount for your success in this field because the scriptwriter must "see" scenes in his head in order to be effective. Thinking about the shots, angles in camera movements are part of this process.

Camera Shots:

- **EWS.** EWS stands for extreme wide shots. This shot is used to establish a scene. The subject is invisible.
- **VWS.** VWS stands for very wide shot. In this type of camera shot, the subject is barely visible but different from the EWS, the emphasis is on the subject.
- **WS.** WS stands for wide shot. In this type of camera shot, the subject is shown in full frame. The wide shot is also referred to as the long shot and can allow character actions.
- **MS.** MS stands for mid shot. In this type of camera shot, only a part of the subject is shown but is more detailed. The subject is shown from waist up. It is considered the common shot.
- **CU.** CU stands for close-up. In this type of camera shot, a particular part of the subject takes the frame, e.g., the subject's head.
- **MCU.** MCU stands for medium close-up. This type of shot can be understood as the shot that shows more subject details than the medium shot. The camera cuts below the shoulder.

- **ECU.** ECU stands for extreme close-up. In this type of camera shot, extreme detail is shown to a point which it would be challenging for the naked eye to see.
- **CA.** CA stands for cue away. In this type of camera shot, the content of the frame is used to fill the scene.
- **Two-Shot.** In this type of camera shot, two people are framed in the frame.
- **OSS.** OSS stands for over-the-shoulder. In this type of camera shot, the camera is placed behind the person the subject is talking to.
- **POV.** POV stands for point of view. In this type of camera shot, the camera shows what the subject is seeing.

Angles

- **Bird's Eye View.** This angle is used to show the audience a view from above. The subject in this type shot is barely visible.
- **High Angle.** The camera is put above the action scene but not as high above as the bird's eye view. The setting becomes the focus and the subject secondary.
- **Eye Level.** The camera is placed at the subject's eye level, which is about 5.5 feet from the ground.
- **Low Angle.** It is often used to confuse the audience. It is used to give actors height.
- **Cantle Angle.** It is the angle type used to create imbalance by tilting the camera.

Camera Movement

- **Tilt.** In tilt, the cameraman moves the camera vertically.
- **Pans.** The cameraman moves the camera horizontally. The subject is in the middle of the frame.
- **Dolly shot.** The camera is placed in a moving device to be able to move along the action of a scene. Sometimes, cars are used in the dolly shot.

- **Hand held.** As the name states, it is when the subject holds a camera.
- **Crane shots.** It is a variation of the dolly shot with the distinction that the camera is placed on a crane, not a car or airplane.
- **Aerial shots.** It is also similar to the dolly shot but is often shot in a helicopter or a remote controlled quad copter. It provides drama to the scene.

QUICK REVIEW

✓ Understanding camera shots is a necessity for novice scriptwriters.
✓ Angles are also crucial for novice scriptwriters.
✓ In a close-up shot, a particular part of the subject takes the whole frame.
✓ In an extreme wide shot, the subject is invisible, which often makes this type of shot the establishing one.
✓ In a two-shot, two people are framed resembling the poses of a medium shot.
✓ In a cut-in shot, other parts of the subject are shown in detail.
✓ Use wide-angle shots to guide your audience to a new scene or action.
✓ Use close-up to get detail of the action.
✓ Use medium shots to bridge between long shots that establish what is happening in the scene.

QUESTIONS

1. In which type of shot is only a part of the subject shown but is more detailed giving the overall impression that part of the subject is in the whole object?
2. In which type of shot does the camera show a view from the subject's perspective?
3. In which type of shot is extreme detail shown?
4. In which type of shot is the subject barely visible but the emphasis is on the subject?
5. Use close-up to get detail of the _____.

SAMPLE EXERCISE (McClelland)

Camera shots and angles are very important in film because they can create a certain mood, help build suspense, and are a window into the story. They really keep the mind wondering and looking at new things. If you held one shot and didn't cut to any different shots then whatever you're filming would be incredibly boring.

Camera angles can create huge amounts of suspense. A good example would come from the famous Alfred Hitchcock film "Vertigo." He did a technique that many filmmakers use. This technique is called the dolly zoom effect. It's basically where you dolly inward and then zoom out at the same pace and vice versa. This camera technique makes the image look like its being stretched or pulled to the outer edges of the frame. Hitchcock did this from high angles to create a sense of height. This really could scare someone if they are acrophobic.

Camera shots and angles are very important during conversations in film. You can cut between the characters to help display emotion and get details of what the character is expressing. Also a tracking shot helps display emotion or reveals important information regarding the story. That tracking shot gives the scene more of a "kick" and adds greatly to the film.

Different types of camera shots signify different meanings. For example, an establishing shot sets up the scene and helps the audience understand where it's taking place. An extreme close-up shot gives extreme detail. There are a variety of camera shots that can be used to affect the way the viewer perceives the subject. It is important for scriptwriters to understand and be able to visualize camera shots if they want to make their scripts into memorable films.

EXERCISE

You are to write for your instructor, in a few pages, why you think camera angles are important for scriptwriters. You must use examples and detailed explanations for your arguments. Make sure you address both camera shots, angles, and camera movements.

5

TERMINOLOGY

"Being used to scientific terminology and theory it was always natural for me to push this stuff into songs." Peter Hammill

LEARNING OBJECTIVES

By the end of the chapter, learners will be able to:

1. Discuss the impact that terminology has on scriptwriting as a career.
2. List three radio broadcasting terms in detail.
3. List three TV broadcasting terms in detail.
4. Explain the similarities between radio and TV scriptwriting.

INTRODUCTION

A competent scriptwriter must know the terminology of the field. Failing to recognize that a scriptwriting lexicon is a must can and probably will result in one of the worse feelings a professional can experience—the fear of "nothing," as I would say—"Nothing comes your way, nothing is fair, nothing happens to me, nothing is given to me." Why should you put yourself in this position? Physicians are quite aware of which terms to use when it comes to treating patients. If you speak with an economist, they also talk "differently" when the matter involves economics. Have you spoken with a computer scientist when the topic is artificial intelligence? Or should I say AI? Or interactions or HCI? See? You need to talk the language of scriptwriters because if you don't, you won't be one. This chapter is about learning the terminology you will find in the field.

TERMINOLOGY FOR RADIO

Different mediums call for different terminology, even though they sometimes overlap. If one is producing a radio show, the terminology could be different than let's say, for TV scriptwriting. It still amazes me that radio scriptwriting is still living in the shadows of TV scriptwriting, especially because of the popularity of talk radio shows. No set is better than the other; they are just different and to be used in different areas, but still you will need to know them. Let me put things in perspective for you. If you want to either pass a course in scriptwriting and/or work in the field of writing scripts for radio (or TV), you will have to learn the terminology used to produce scripts. Without knowing it, you will not have even a chance of making it in the field—trust me. Let's get our hands wet and start learning the terms in the field of radio scriptwriting and study the definitions provided by Straczynski (1997).

- **actuality.** Actuality is often referred to as a sound bite. It is actually a recorded speech delivered by a professional news person that usually lasts 15 seconds.
- **clock.** This term is used in radio scriptwriting to indicate the radio broadcast hour with precise minutes and seconds of time.
- **cut.** The "cut" is basically a device containing an audio recording delivered by a person. With modern computer technology nowadays, "cuts" are delivered to station affiliates through satellite transmission.
- **hourly.** This term indicates that the radio broadcast will start at the top of the hour. It often finishes five minutes before the next hour and typically includes announcements and preparation for the top of the next hour.
- **IQ.** IQ stands for in cue and are the first words you will see on a cut.

- **lead.** The best way to understand what a "lead" is is to think beginnings, or should we say the very first sentence you will find in a news story delivered through radio. Basically, the "lead" has to reveal, inductively, the story's basic events and introduce what the show will be about for the remaining of the broadcast.
- **live shot.** A live shot is exactly what it says it is. It is a report delivered by a radio professional that is being delivered live and hasn't been recorded before.
- **lockout.** The lockout is the final spoken words a radio professional says prior to the end of his show. The professional is to give his name and station's frequency or acronym. An example could be, "Thank you for listening to the Dr. A show here at WIUP 90.1FM."
- **MOS.** MOS stands for "Man On The Street" interviews. The typical scenario for MOS is when a professional randomly chooses folks to be interviewed in public.
- **nat.** This term is any sound that isn't recorded by a radio voice or guest. Sounds of keyboard typing or thunder are examples of a "Nat."
- **OQ.** OQ stands for "out cue" or the last words you will see recorded on a cut or the device containing an audio recording delivered by a person.
- **reader.** The reader is basically a story read by an anchor with no screen graphic.
- **script.** A script is what is read on the air by an announcer.
- **slug.** The slug is the script's title, which is often used as a reference.
- **sounder.** The music used to introduce beginnings and ends of radio broadcasts.
- **spot.** An advertisement filed on tape.
- **tease.** Teases, prior to commercial breaks, are short phrases spoken by an announcer.
- **voicer.** A voicer is a pre-recorded work of an announcer's voice.
- **wrap.** A kind of radio story that has the anchor lead followed by a reporter's voice with the actual sound bite. It is a radio packaged story.
- **zinger.** Funny story at the end of a newscast.

TERMINOLOGY FOR TV

TV script language is extensive. In this section, I will provide a number of terms that you should be able to use in your projects. However, it won't be a complete one, as there are books dedicated to this task alone. I will make this section as concise as I can yet provide as many terms as I think you should know. I encourage you to go out and investigate! There is nothing wrong with increasing your knowledge of scriptwriting, especially if you go to the library. Let me tell you a secret. The societies of the future are likely to be based on the principles of the past. Go to the library and get an old book about TV scriptwriting terminology, and you will quickly realize that the "modern" world is simply mimicking what was done 50 years back. See? Dr. A is also wisdom! Anyway, let's get back to task here; let's talk about TV script terminology according to Straczynski (1997).

- **boom shot.** This term refers to high-angle shots under camera movement conditions.
- **cutaway.** It is a kind of shot that is shot far away from the actual TV scene.
- **cuts.** It is a term to indicate a quick change from one scene to another.
- **dolly.** This is a term often used when the actual camcorder is moving away or towards the actor.
- **Dutch angle shot.** It is a type of camera shot that is tilted between 25–45 degrees to either side causing the horizon to be at a particular angle.
- **establishing shots.** It is also referred to as a wide shot and gives the viewers an understanding about the environment.
- **EXT.** EXT in TV scriptwriting stands for exterior.
- **fade-in.** It is a two-second transition from a blank (black screen) to picture.
- **fade-out.** It is a two-second transition from a picture to a blank (black screen).
- **full shot (FS).** It is a camera shot where the cameraman captures the shot from head to feet, at the bare minimum.

- **insert shot.** The best way to explain "insert shot" is to think about a scene. It is really a close-up of an object or parts of the body in a scene.
- **INT.** In TV scriptwriting, INT stands for interior.
- **lap-dissolves.** Lap-dissolves is a transition term in TV scriptwriting to indicate the two scenes overlapped from one scene to another.
- **long shot (LS).** Same as full shot.
- **master shot.** This type of camera shot is also referred as a clone to the establishing shot.
- **medium shot (MS).** It is a camera shot focused from the waist up of a subject.
- **MOC.** Man on camera.
- **MOT.** Man on tape.
- **moving shot.** They are also referred as tracking shots in TV scripting, which basically means that the camera moves a bit during the actual footage capture/scene.
- **OS (over-the-shoulder shot).** It is a camera shot where the camera is placed at the back of an actor's head and/or shoulder.
- **POV (point of view).** It is a camera shot where the focus is on the view of the actor. Imagine a video game where you can see the track inside of a car. It is a point of view shot.
- **SFX (special effects).** It can be understood as the term for both video and/or special effect.
- **SIL.** Silent tape.
- **SOT.** Sound on tape.
- **subjective shot.** It is a camera shot where the viewer will see what the actor is seeing.
- **takes.** A take is basically a segment of a scene with various elements.
- **three-shot (3-S).** It is a camera shot with three people in the actual scene.
- **truck.** It is referred to as a lateral camera move in TV scriptwriting.
- **two-shot (2-S).** It is a camera shot with two people in the actual scene.

- **VO (Voice over).** Stands for voice over narration heard through background music or sound.
- **XCU.** It is a camera shot designed to produce a dramatic effect.
- **zoom.** Bringing the subject closer or further from the camera.

REVIEW CHECKLIST

✓ Failing to recognize that a scriptwriting lexicon is a must can and probably will result in one of the worst feelings a professional can experience—the fear of "nothing" as I would say—"Nothing comes your way, nothing is fair, nothing happens to me, nothing is given to me."

✓ Actuality is often referred to as a sound bite. It is recorded speech delivered by a professional news person that usually lasts 15 seconds.

✓ IQ stands for in cue and are the first words you will see on a cut.

✓ A live shot is exactly what it says it is. It is a report delivered by a radio professional that is being delivered live and hasn't been recorded before.

✓ Establishing shots are also referred to as wide shots to give the viewers an understanding about the environment.

✓ Fade-in is a two-second transition from a blank (black screen) to picture.

✓ Fade-out is a two-second transition from a picture to a blank (black screen).

QUESTIONS

1. Provide reasons to why you should know scriptwriting terminology in your career.
2. What is the difference between a fade-in and a fade-out shot?
3. Which terminology can you think of that can be used in both radio and TV?
4. When do you think you should use a fade-in and/or a fade-out?

SAMPLE EXERCISE (Mason)

A man is standing outside of a bus garage and is slightly jet-lagged after he gets off the bus. An establishing shot pans down and sets the theme of the story. It is cold and damp out and the man is agitated because he was crammed in the bus. After the establishing shot we have a sequence of shots explaining the type of the weather. It is cold and he is basically alone. The man is getting agitated and, we have a series of CU shots focused on his forehead, eyes, and hands. You can tell that he is fidgeting and he is pacing. He is waiting for a very important ride and a small black bag that is basically glued to his hands accompanies him. He looks over his shoulder and we have a POV shot followed by an OS shot. He is getting really paranoid now.

The second series of shots is focusing on how nervous he is. Everything starts slowing down. POV shots looking left to right very fast . . . frantic . . . . Beads of sweat follow a dolly shot of sweat falling to the ground. We see a bead individually in slow motion and have a medium CU of the bead, and as it hits the ground time goes back to normal. Superimposition and fade through white of a close-up of the man's distraught pale face follows after. Finally he hears the faint rumbling of the car and we are directed with an OS shot. He is finally at ease for a brief second, and we see an aerial shot of a car moving towards him. A dolly shot from left to right brings the car into the scene. We see the man run to the car and he gets in very fast. The LS of the man getting into the car is followed by a POV shot of something looking at the man from a distance with a slightly obstructed view. The shot is hand-held and we see some movement. Cut to inside the car and we hear the first dialogue. The man asks what took you so long to the woman? (OS) She says don't worry about it and drives off out of the scene from a medium shot of the car and then a long shot of them leaving the scene. We then go back to the mysterious POV shot of something watching them, and the shot dollies down the street after the car. We are brought back into the scene with an OS shot inside the car with the man and woman. The man keeps checking his watch. He is really in a panic now. He is grabbing his bag now and they are on a bridge. We

see them following a car down the bridge with a LS that is being dol-
lied by a helicopter showing a partial aerial shot. Cut to a parade in
the downtown with lots of people watching floats go by. Cut to the
car, CU on the woman's foot who slams on the gas just as she is exit-
ing the bridge. We are now back to the obstructed point of view, and it
shows a dark figure jumping in front of the car. Cut to the man and
woman in the car. The man starts screaming that it's him, it is him.
The woman swerves out of the way and charges towards the busy city.
Cut to the man who is moving the handle up and down saying let me
out. The woman responds no. The man tucks and rolls out of the car
leaving his small black bag. We cut to the driver focusing on her face
and then a POV shot as she opens the bag and sees a timer. We cut to
an ECU of the woman's eyes as they get very large and her pupils
dilate. Oh SHIIIIIIIIIIIIIIIIIIIIIIIIII...................We hear a large explosion
and cut to black..........After the pan dollies up we see the destruction
of the bomb, and through the rubble we see the obstructed POV shot
walking towards the car. He walks up to the man and he is screaming.
We see a CU of the man screaming saying NOOOOOOO......Then we
zoom in all the way and fade to white, still hearing the man's scream.

SAMPLE EXERCISE (Ranish)

"A man is waiting for someone along the road. The man is getting
increasingly annoyed as time passes. He looks at a watch and paces
back and forth. A woman finally drives up . . . he enters the car and
drives away with the woman."

1. *Fade in* from black to an *establishing shot* of an outdoor scene
   of a town; include in the shot the position of the sun so we
   know what time of day it is.
2. *Cut* to a *long shot* of a well dressed but scruffy man standing
   alongside a road.
3. *Cut in* to a *close-up* of the man's face looking bored and rub-
   bing his chin to imply that he is waiting for something.

4. Use the *fade transition,* to show a passage of time, to a *medium shot* of the man sitting on the curb.

5. As the man turns his head to the right to look down the road, *cut* to a *POV.*

6. *Cut* back to the *medium shot* of the man.

7. As the man turns his head to the left, *cut* to another *POV.*

8. *Cut* back to the *medium shot* of the man again.

9. *Fade* to a *medium long shot* of the man standing again.

10. From the *MLS,* as the man looks at his watch, *cut in* to a *close-up* of the watch.

11. As the man puts his arm back down by his side, *pan down* with the arm all the way down to his foot to see it tapping anxiously.

12. *Cut* to an *extreme close-up* to his eyes.

13. *Cut* to a *long shot* of him standing and then starting to pace back and forth.

14. After he starts pacing, *cut in* to a *medium close-up* of just his feet moving.

15. *Cut* back to a *medium long shot.*

16. *Cut away* to a *close-up* of a car tire moving and the camera *panning* with it.

17. *Cut away* to a *close-up* of the man's face turning at presumably the sound of a car.

18. *Cut away* to a *medium long shot* of a car driving away from the camera and where the man can be seen in the shot.

19. *Cut* to a *medium shot* of the man from behind and the car pulling up in front of him.

20. *Cut* to a *POV* from the man as he bends slightly to look in the window of the car and sees the woman.

21. *Cut* to a *POV* from the woman looking back at the man.

22. *Cut* to a *close-up* of the man opening the door.

23. *Cut* to a *medium shot* from behind the car of the man getting in and then the car driving away.

24. *Fade* out to black.

EXERCISE

In order to practice scriptwriting, let's use the shots and transitions discussed in this chapter. Let's not worry about formatting yet, since it will come in the next chapter but nonetheless, let's practice. Apply the terms (conceptually) you were exposed to in this chapter along with the following scenario.

"A man is waiting for someone along the road. The man is getting increasingly annoyed as time passes. He looks at a watch and paces back and forth. A woman finally drives up . . . he enters and drives away with the woman."

6

INTERVIEWING

"An investigation may take six months. A quick interview, profile, a day." Diane Sawyer

LEARNING OBJECTIVES

By the end of the chapter, learners will be able to:

1. List three techniques for conducting successful scriptwriting interviews.
2. Explain why interviews are important.
3. Conduct professional interviews.
4. Differentiate between good and bad interviews.

PRIOR TO INTERVIEWING

The interview, contrary to what folks believe, does not start at the interview date. It starts prior to the interview when you organize your thoughts, conceptualize a plan of action, and do what you can to look prepared and professional. You are to think about your audience before you think about the interview and the interviewee since your story will be seen by your audience after all. You should start by doing some investigation about what you are trying to cover before asking any questions of somebody. You are, however, to think about possible questions you could ask in order to capture information to help tell your story.

WHY IS INTERVIEWING IMPORTANT?

The interview is an important component of scriptwriting because it allows you to get information as well as sound bites to be used in your script story. You are to be courteous and sensitive to your interviewee's behavioral responses; don't forget that. After all, they will help you tremendously with your story. There are a large number of tips you can receive when it comes to scriptwriting and interviewing. In the next section, I will discuss a few of them with you providing a correspondent explanation.

INTERVIEW TIPS

Interviewing is an art and it should be mastered if you want to be a known scriptwriter for any medium, e.g., TV and radio. In this section, I will discuss a few techniques and tips you can use to maximize your data gathering. Let's have some fun!

- **Do prior investigations.** You must know some information in advance, e.g., who is the person you are interviewing, their background, etc. By doing this, you will make it clear to the interviewee that you did your homework and eventually, this will have an impact during the interview.
- **Start introducing yourself.** Introduce yourself to the interviewee. Establish rapport and reduce the tension between you, the circumstance, and him.
- **Ask open ended questions.** Let the interviewee talk and don't interrupt. Ask their opinions about a subject, not whether something is or is not. Avoid yes/no questions. They aren't good ones for scriptwriting interview protocols when using an open ended format.
- **Record your interview.** It is virtually impossible to gather all the data from either a structured and/or unstructured interview the first time you listen. You must have a recording device to help you with data collection, especially because of accuracy and

ratification issues. Don't forget, however, to ask the interviewee if it is okay to record the interview.

- **Take notes.** What happens if your recording device does not work after your interview? You will lose it all, right? WRONG! If you take notes, you will have some data to finish your project and/or guide you to get the remaining information you need. Make sure you bring the medium with the highest resolution (paper) and a pencil with you at the time of the interview.
- **Help them ask questions.** Sometimes interviewees don't answer your questions but it isn't because they don't want to. Have you ever thought that perhaps, they just don't understand what you are asking? You could, in circumstances like these, rephrase your questions and see if the interviewee replies to what you want to cover. Don't be shy to even deviate to your questions a bit in order to gather the data.
- **Keep probing but pay attention.** Don't end your interview until you gather the information you need. However, you must be sensitive to the interviewees time and nonverbal behaviors. If he is looking at the door, the window, or his watch, it is perhaps time to wrap up the interview as these are indicators of uneasiness and anxiety.
- **Use a conversational style.** People like to talk; therefore, let them talk! Act as if you are having a conversation with a friend. The more you do this, the better information you will get for your scripts.
- **First questions are paramount.** The first few questions of your interview will determine the interviewees perceptions about you and how much he will cooperate. My advice? Ask great questions in the beginning of your session.
- **Treat people well.** Treat others as they deserve. Who wants to be treated badly? Would you like to be treated with disrespect? Remember, you need their responses in order to have a story.
- **Avoid bubble gum and constant movements.** Under no circumstances chew gum and/or keep moving around constantly during a scriptwriting interview.

REVIEW CHECKLIST

- ✓ Contrary to what folks believe, a good interview does not start at the interview date. It starts prior to the interview when you organize your thoughts, conceptualize a plan of action, and do what you can to look prepared and professional.
- ✓ You are to think about possible questions you could ask in order to capture information to help you tell your story.
- ✓ Under no circumstances chew gum and/or keep moving around constantly during a scriptwriting interview.
- ✓ The interview is an important component of scriptwriting because it allows you to get information as well as sound bites to be used in your script story.
- ✓ Introduce yourself to the interviewee. Establish rapport and reduce the tension between you, the circumstance, and him.
- ✓ Don't end your interview until you gathered the information you need. However, you must be sensitive to the interviewees time and nonverbal behaviors.
- ✓ Use a conversational style.

QUESTIONS

1. Which background information should you get prior to interviewing somebody?
2. Let's assume that you were approached by a reporter to give him your opinions about a subject matter but he disregarded you. What would you do in this situation?
3. Why should you present great questions at first?
4. Would you probe your interviewee? Defend your position.
5. What is the role of your audience in a scriptwriting interview?

SAMPLE EXERCISE (Mason)

I chose to conduct my interview with my Aunt Elaine about our family history and what her childhood was like. She lives in Deltona, FL, and the interview was conducted last Wednesday and was conducted over the phone. The interview was set for 45 minutes but lasted a little over one hour.

1. **What is your full name? Why did your parents select this name for you? Do you have any nicknames?**

A: My Aunt **Elaine Marie Demas-Beaumont-Haley** was named after her paternal grandmother and maternal grandmother and was born on January 7th, 1949. Her paternal grandmother's name was Helen Demas. Helen can be translated from Greek to Eleni and from that came Elaine. Her middle name refers to her maternal grandmother whose name was Mary (Mary Manos), which can be translated from Greek to Maria which also can be used for the name Marie. Over the years she has always been called Elaine but when she was in nursing school she was nicknamed Miss Elaine, which then turned to her nickname Miss-Elainious. She has always liked her name, and coincidence or not many of her close friends have shared the same name with her.

2. **When and where were you born?**

A: Aunt Elaine was born in the Sewickly Hospital in Sewickly, PA. A story that she shared when she was born was about her Father (George Demas) mistaking her for the wrong baby in another crib. He asked to see his baby and the nurse brought an African American child to him because of his darker Mediterranean complexion, and after that he corrected the nurse that she brought him the wrong child.

3. **Were there other family members in the area? Who?**

A: Elaine had the good fortune to have a very close relationship with her paternal grandparents John and Helen Demas. The family shared an apartment with them and lived upstairs. When she was little she referred to them as upstairs Yia-yia and Pappou (grandmother and grandfather in Greek). This gave Elaine constant access to her grandparents. They were very involved in her childhood and would walk her to school and also walk in downtown Ambridge. When she was in second grade her family moved from the apartment to a house on 623 Steele Street. Her family was among the first families to move away from the area where all the family lived. They were only 5 miles away but this was a big deal to the family.

4. What was your house like?

A: Elaine recalled that they were the only family to have a flat yard even though they lived on a very big hill. Behind their house they had access to woods where she spent a lot of time building cabins in the woods and making perfume from locust blossoms. She sometimes had to "borrow" some perfume from her mother to make it smell better. She also informed me about how she spent a lot of time at her neighbor Judy's house drawing their own cutout dolls and designing clothes. There was also a birdbath at her friend's house and this is a calming totem that she has had at every house she has ever lived in since then, because it takes her back to her childhood and reminds her of security and peacefulness. She did not have many warm memories of the house on Steele Street because of her mother's strict rules.

5. What was your favorite toy?

A: Elaine had a very special possession and that was her doll Beauty. She got the doll when she was still living in the apartment with her paternal grandparents near Merchant Street. She really wanted the doll for Christmas but her father was unemployed at the time so she wasn't expecting the doll. Her grandfather took the last bus the night before Christmas to the shopping center and got the doll. Since it was the last bus he had to walk all the way home, nearly 7 miles. She still has the doll to this very day and has had it repaired to fix the hair. The doll has the original bathrobe but the other clothes are still MIA.

6. **Did you have family chores? What were they? What was the worst?**

A: Elaine vividly remembers the chores that she did around the house. It was mainly cleaning because her mother Virginia Demas did the laundry and cooking. Elaine did not dread chores because they were a natural part of the housekeeping routine. She would wax cabinets and dust every Wednesday and Friday. The chores were very rigid and strict. The family was not allowed to have fun or do anything until the chores were done, and Virginia would be the enforcer. One time Elaine was cleaning for so long her Aunt Helen came and rescued her and took her from the house so she could stop cleaning. Virginia would help her memorize bible verses while they cleaned.

7. **Were there any fads? What was your favorite?**

A: Elaine is very family oriented because of the things she did as a child. Some of the things she remembered as popular were going to the movies as a family to see flicks like, "The King and I" and "Oklahoma." Two fads that she did not like were saddle shoes and a perm that her mother made her get.

8. **What was a typical vacation like?**

A: Elaine's favorite vacation was going to Wildwood, NJ, every year. This was the entire family's favorite place to go because the fishing was good, which John and George enjoyed, and the beach was nice, which the girls enjoyed a lot! They had some cousins there and they would see them every year. Her father George stressed the importance of a family vacation. "No matter what you should always go on vacation as a family once a year," he would say.

The typical day of vacation started early in the morning when the family would wake up early and have breakfast followed by making lunch and food to take to the beach with them. They packed the cooler every day and enjoyed picnics on the beach. Fishing was involved as well as swimming and other beach activities. After they stayed at the beach till about 5 pm they would get very dressed up in dresses and nice clothes and go to a local restaurant called Dom's. Following dinner they would walk the boardwalk at night and look at the shops. They did this ritual every night of the vacation. One year they brought their grandfather John and he was very funny to see with sunglasses on and rolled up pants on the beach. One day Elaine and her father went to every store on the boardwalk looking for a Barbie doll for her sister Maria for her birthday. They never found one but got one on their return to Pittsburgh.

9. **What was a typical family dinner like?**

A: A typical family dinner consisted of a large family meal that was usually served in the kitchen. The meal was traditional in the sense that a meat, vegetable, and salad, potatoes, and a dessert were served. Virginia did all of the cooking and was known for creating many cuisines in the pressure cooker with some sort of tomato based sauce. They always had chicken on Sunday and would eat as a family after church with extended family. The food was all made from scratch and was very nutritious and healthy.

10. **Are there any recipes that have been passed down to you?**

A: Elaine learned to cook from both of her grandmothers. She really enjoyed baking and is still very interested in baking sugar cookies around the holidays. She has passed many of her talents to her daughter Jeannie Haury. One thing about the family recipes over the years is that Greek people do not like to share recipes with others and will often leave out certain ingredients. This comes from an old saying that the recipes stay in the family and are not to be shared. Elaine would write down the recipes as her grandmother cooked. A half eggshell full of water was then recorded as 1 tablespoon. She deciphered the techniques and came up with recipes from her mother and grandmothers. She could never figure out why her mother's Greek lasagna was a different orange color and then she found out her mother did not rinse the sauce off of the spoon before she stirred the crème sauce. Also doing the sign of the cross and implicating religion while cooking so that God would bless the food was also common practice while cooking with her family.

11. What was your favorite holiday and why?

A: Elaine's favorite holiday was a tie between Christmas and New Year's. A typical Christmas consisted of her father filming the children coming down the steps on Christmas morning in their new pajamas from their grandmother Mary. The films show that they were usually spanked because they were doing bad things before they came down because they were so excited. They would open gifts as their dad filmed them, and they would always get an Easter dress from their Aunt Helen, Virginia's sister. Some traditions were putting a dollar bill on the tree every year and then collecting them and not spending them. The new bill would magically appear on the tree and it was tradition to put them on the tree after the ornaments were all on.

Another favorite holiday for Elaine was New Year's. A tradition that was common on New Year's was that the first guest of the New Year to enter your house was the bringer of luck. So you would give them a dollar for bringing your home good luck. In Greek it is called the "Aspro Pothy" or white foot (rabbits foot). Another tradition was to hit your grandparent in the head with an orange. She was not sure how it became tradition or what it meant but they did it every year.

My Aunt Elaine is very involved in our family history and has done a lot of research on ancestry.com. It is very cool because she has so much information and has spent countless hours making sure that our family history does not fade away. I commend her for all the hard work she has done and how her research will make sure our family is always together.

EXERCISE

Interviewing is a critical component of scriptwriting. You are to conduct a thirty minute interview with a classmate and write down the questions along with the whole transcript. Make sure to use as many tips presented in this chapter as possible.

7

VIGNETTE

"We are trying to show little vignettes of things you normally wouldn't see every day." Nancy Lynch

LEARNING OBJECTIVES

By the end of the chapter, learners will be able to:

1. Describe what a vignette is.
2. Name the criteria for writing a vignette.
3. Explain why you should write vignettes if you want to be a scriptwriter.
4. Construct a word diagram to help you write vignettes.

WHAT IS A VIGNETTE?

In scriptwriting, a vignette is a short but vigorous piece of writing that leaves you with an impression of a scene. The vignette is to focus on a moment, giving an impression about an idea, character, or setting. A vignette is not to be confused with a treatment. In fact, we will be talking about treatments in the next chapter. If you are looking for a position in scriptwriting, you will need to be a vignette master writer!

WHY SHOULD WE PRACTICE VIGNETTES?

Practicing writing vignettes should make you a better thinker and, consequently, a better writer. When I was a teenager, I had a beautiful girlfriend by the name of Andrea. She always wanted to be an artist but like most teenagers, she didn't know how. Therefore, she decided to go back to her elementary school and ask the sister why she couldn't draw as well as her friends in high school. The sister replied back with a single sentence that I know immediately changed her life. The sister replied, "Daughter, you are not an artist because you don't practice." Andrea was speechless, went home, and started practicing. To make a long story short, she became an artist.

EXAMPLE OF HOW TO WRITE A VIGNETTE

Scriptwriters write vignettes differently. The method I am going to show you is not the only way to write vignettes but it is just one way. Are you ready to write great vignettes? Alright, let's get started.

- Start by thinking about a topic to write about. Let's say the topic is "Routine."
- Write whatever you want to write about on a piece of paper and place it in the center of the page.
- Start drawing boxes connecting them with lines making sure that the words you choose are related to "routine" in this example.
- Connect the words you came up with.
- Construct your own diagram of ideas. Make sure you draw the diagram. Having a "mental" diagram is not good enough.
- Start writing, looking at the words you came up with.
- Revise your writing.

EXAMPLE OF A SCRIPTED VIGNETTE

INT. IUP STOUFFER FLOOR—NIGHT

Vignette of Dr. P: Through the building's door, we move in on Dr. P looking down a long hall. Close-up to Dr. P blinking his right eye and taking off his glasses.

Dr. P (V.O.)

Prior to being a physician, I was a great administrator. I worked as a college provost for twelve years helping institutions becoming better financially. It is amazing how life is so unpredictable. I can't believe that I am now the chair of a department in Communications.

INT. IUP GAME LAB—NIGHT

Vignette of Dr. A: Sitting at his desk, typing a word document, drinking a glass of soda, and smoking a cigar. LS to Dr. A smiling and thinking deeply.

Dr. A (V.O.)

WOW, here I am at IUP as a college professor. Life is good, my cigar tastes great, I love life. Man, I wish I had more soda in my refrigerator.

REVIEW CHECKLIST

- ✓ The first step in writing a vignette is to start by thinking about a topic to write about.
- ✓ In scriptwriting, a vignette is a short but vigorous piece of writing that leaves you with an impression of a scene.
- ✓ A vignette is not to be confused with a treatment.
- ✓ Write whatever you want to write about on a piece of paper and place it in the center of the page.
- ✓ The vignette is to focus on a moment giving an impression about an idea, character, or setting.

QUESTIONS

1. Which terms could you use to format your vignette script?
2. Tell your group, in a few words, what a vignette is.
3. Why are writing vignettes important for the novice scriptwriter?
4. What should you do to write vignettes?
5. What does (V.O.) stand for?

SAMPLE EXERCISES (Mason)

Vignettes are very curious parts of scriptwriting and are among the basic fundamentals. Vignettes can be used in all aspects of multimedia productions. They are usually one of the first stepping-stones when creating media projects such as commercials, promos, or other advertising materials. A vignette could be considered a short story that describes a scene, and when it is scripted you add camera angles to the scene.

Vignette #1 (Scripted)

The day in the life of a disc golfer

The scene opens with a title explaining a day of disc golf and then cuts to a time lapse of the group driving to the disc golf course (ES). The friends get out of the SUV (WS) and make their way to hole 1(DS). They set their bags on the ground and begin some arm stretches to warm up their arms (MS). The first of three get ready to throw their drive (WS to MS). They all throw their first discs and make it more than half the way to the hole (LS), except one of the friends hits a tree with his opening shot and his disc falls to the ground (MCU). Their second shots are all thrown and they are approximately 10 feet to the basket (WS). Friend 1 throws his shot (POV) and sinks the put. We hear chains and the disc rests in the basket (CU). Friend 2 throws his shot and it also makes it in (DS). The pressure is on the final subject (CA). He is nervous but approaches the basket (CUT-IN). He goes to throw and releases the disc (POV). Everything slows down and we watch the disc hit the chains (ECU). The disc falls in the basket and excitement comes over the subject. The friends all high five and then continue to the next hole. We have an ES with the basket in view and the friends continuing on the path (VWS).

Vignette #2 (Scripted)

Pond Fishing

We open to a scene at a pond in the middle of the woods (ES). Two people are fishing on a rudimentary dock that is made out of wood (OSS). They are casting with spinning reels into the large pond (MS). It is about 10:00 in the morning as we see a close-up of one subject's watch on his hand as he goes out to release a cast that lands 25 feet from the dock (ECU to CU). His bobber hits the water with a small splash and then bobs in the water with the bait on the other end (CU). We see a close-up of the bobber as it flickers in the water. There is something on the other end as it plunges below the surface (CU). We then have a POV shot as the man jerks back on his rod to set the hook. He starts reeling as the rod bends towards the water (POV). The bobber is getting closer, and we can see the fish thrashing below the surface (CUT-IN). The man reels in all the way and grabs the end of his line hoisting his prize in the air (Dolly to WS).

Vignette #3

Opening Day

An alarm sounds in a dark room and the lights turn on. A man grabs his backpack and all of the hunting gear lying next to the floor. He is ready for a hunt. He heads down to the stairs of his apartment and throws the gear in the bed of his truck. He heads down the highway to his prosperous hunting ground. He gears up before first light, and we can see how cold it is out because you can see his breath. The truck door slams and the hunter heads up the windy path to his destination. He hikes up hill and downhill and enters on a shallow game trial. It is still dark out so he shines his flashlight that illuminates a small reflective button on the tree. He keeps on his path and follows the next illumination button. Walking down the trail he is finally near his stand. He attaches his gear to a rope and climbs into the tree and then pulls up his gear. It is now first light and he is looking over a cornfield. He uses his rattle bag and rustles it to call in a deer. The hunter waits eagerly as he waits for the animal.

Vignette #4

Mountain Biking

Two bikes greet us by flying past the camera. The camera switches positions and shows them as they continue down the trail. It is shady because they are under the cover of the leaves, but when they move out of the shade and drive past a cornfield they are illuminated in the high noon sun. Moving down the trail they ride over a bridge, and it brings them at a crossroads. They cross the road and meander down the dirt trail. We then have a handlebar view of the real action that is going on as they speed over bumps and sticks. They skid on a patch of loose dirt and make a sharp turn. We then have a wide shot of the group riding past a river. They decide to stop and rest on a flat rock jutting out by the river and grab a quick snack of trail mix for an energy boost. They are now on their way and pull into a canoe rental space. They exchange their bike locks for paddles and get ready for their canoeing adventure.

Vignette #5

Bonfires

Split wood hits the ground after an ax swings all the way through the log. Wood is falling all over the place as the main subject swings away at dried oak logs. He is getting ready for a fire and is prepping his kindling. He stacks his wood next to the pit and begins to create the framework of the fire. He lays sticks across in a tic-tac-toe pattern and then places a fine nest of small wood in the direct center. He strikes a match on a box and tosses it into the center of the frame. The ball of tinder ignites as the fire engulfs the frame of wood and then he frantically feeds the fire with larger sticks and keeps getting bigger ones to add to the fire. It is now roaring with flames, and the man gets a piece of flimsy plywood and begins to fan the fire, giving it new life as flames lick around the logs. He then sits and breaks open his hotdogs, and sits back relaxing while he admires the blanket of stars above him.

SAMPLE EXERCISES (Denio)

"Ice Cream"

Sarah excitedly drives to an ice cream parlor after a long day at work. When she goes inside she sees that there is a long line, but decides to wait anyway since she has been looking forward to her special treat all day. After waiting for twenty minutes, she orders two scoops of cookie dough ice cream in a bowl and leaves. When she gets to her parked car, she places the ice cream on the roof so she can unlock the door. She gets inside her car and drives away. To her dismay, Sarah realizes moments later that she left her ice cream on the roof! So much for that special treat.

"Mystery Package"

Fade in from black.

[A woman wearing dark sunglasses and trench coat arrives in front of a private residence.]

Cut to a full shot of the woman standing in front of the private residence.

Cut to a wide shot of the house and the land surrounding it.

[She walks toward the front door holding a small package wrapped in brown paper.]

Cut to medium shot of the woman, showing her face, as she walks toward the door.

Cut to a close-up of the package the woman is holding.

Cut to a full shot of the front door

[When she arrives at the door, she places the package on the step, knocks on the door twice, and quickly leaves.]

Cut to a wide shot of the residence and the woman standing at the door.

Cut to a medium shot showing the woman placing the package on the step.

Cut to a close-up of the woman's hand as she knocks twice.

Cut to a wide shot showing the woman leaving quickly.

[The owner of the residence opens the door and picks up the package and reads an attached note with the message, "Do not open."]

Cut to a full shot of the front door opening and the owner of the house.

Cut to a medium shot of the man reaching down to pick up the package.

Cut to a close-up shot of the man's face as he looks at the package and sees the note.

Cut to a subjective insert shot of the note.

Cut to a wide shot of the residence and the man standing outside with a puzzled look on is face.

Fade to black.

"Unemployment"

"Alex loses his job as an office worker after the company goes bankrupt. For three months he is unemployed and spends his days standing around and doing nothing. Finally after searching and searching, the only job he is able to find is working as a mannequin. It pays very little, but it is better than standing around for free."

"Starting Over"

Fade in from black.

[Lydia arrives at the train station with her suitcase in hand, anxiously anticipating the start of her new life abroad.]

Cut to wide shot of the train station, also showing the woman as she arrives and walks towards the platform.

Cut to close-up of the woman's face as she smiles.

Cut to medium shot showing the woman's bottom half and her suitcases.

[The train arrives at 3 o'clock sharp.]

Cut to close-up of clock striking 3 o'clock

Cut to wide shot of the train arriving.

[She gets onto the train, finds her seat, and sits down.]

Cut to medium shot of the woman walking on the train and sitting in her seat.

[As the train departs, she stares out the window and watches as the only place she ever knew becomes a place of the past.]

Cut to close-up shot of the woman's face as she stares out the window.

Cut to subjective insert shot of the scenery outside of the window.

[She opens a small journal kept in her purse and writes, "I will miss that place, but can never return for no one can ever find out I killed that man."]

Cut to medium shot of woman taking journal out of purse.

Cut to close-up of woman's face as she writes.

Cut to subjective insert shot of the journal showing what the woman wrote.

Fade to black.

"Lost and Found"

"A lost Labrador Retriever named Samson walks along an abandoned railroad, searching for his owner—searching for his home. He looks here and there, sniffing out any traces of his best friend, but comes up short. Samson is hungry and tired; he dreams of curling up in his soft bed with a full stomach. The dog nearly gives up when he hears a familiar whistle in the distance. He runs toward the sound and is elated to see his owner running toward him. Samson runs to his owner and both man and dog are overjoyed to finally be reunited once again."

EXERCISE

You are to write five vignettes based on the example shown below. Make sure you script at least five vignettes.

> *"A man gets up in the morning, goes to the bathroom and shaves. He leaves his house, stops at a Stop and Go and buys a cup of coffee. After buying the coffee, he gets into his car and continues to work. He arrives, goes inside an office building, goes to his desk, and sits."*

8

TREATMENT

"No, I can't write treatments, I think there's a danger with treatments. That you . . . you write out your first excitement and enthusiasm in a prose treatment." Ronald Hardwood

LEARNING OBJECTIVES

By the end of the chapter, learners will be able to:

1. Explain what a treatment is.
2. Discuss what should be included in a treatment.
3. Name the criteria for writing a treatment.
4. Analyze treatments and provide critical feedback.

WHAT IS IT?

A treatment is a basic script theme also known as a story-idea. It can be written up to ten pages long, not in outlying format but as a general story plot. Basically, you are to pick apart an idea and explain it in detail. A treatment is an important piece of scriptwriting work because it can be used to display your idea prior to fully immersing yourself in an endeavor that might not be funded or published. A writing treatment for a scriptwriter is like recording a quick demo of a song for a recording company. The piece should be a piece of your work but comprehensive enough to give yourself a shot to be funded or, in the case of the music industry, recorded.

WHAT IS TO BE INCLUDED?

In the treatment, you are to include the description of the main character of your story and the scenes that will be included. Make sure that you smooth the language almost as if you were writing a short story. Choose sophisticated words to keep the reader interested in your treatment. You should also provide a concise summary of what is to be included in your treatment and how it will be developed over time. Think of writing treatments as a way to get funds for your projects and have a job. Understanding that a reviewer will be analyzing your work and that he/she might have certain expectations about acceptance can help you with delivering what they want to receive. Don't forget that.

TREATMENT FORMAT

The treatment must be written in a specific format if you want your project to receive fair consideration. You must write the treatment in third person (he/she), in present tense, and in narrative format. DO NOT use past tense, first person, and/or bullet points. Your project won't be funded if you decide to make these decisions. You are to also explain your project in detail, with a specialized outline emphasizing drama and communicating excitement to the client.

SAMPLE TREATMENT

Sludge waste utilization is an issue of growing concern to the residents of Indiana County, Pennsylvania. In the fall of 1985, the subject was brought to the public's attention at hearings where residents sought legal means to prevent sludge utilization at several locations. Their primary concern is the concentration of lead and other toxic metals in sludge that may eventually leak into local water supplies. Though as yet there have been no documented cases of poisoning resulting from sludge utilization, the residents are very concerned.

The purpose of this documentary is to educate the public on the facts surrounding the issue and to use Indiana County as an example of a community faced with making a decision on the issue.

The program will first endeavor to catch the audience's attention by presenting brief general statements on the subject by people to be interviewed later in the program. A narrator will be used to present background on the subject. This will include a definition of sludge waste, explaining its origins and contents. Any scientific information will be kept in simple terms for comprehension.

Next, the methods of disposal will be presented with the subject of utilization being brought into focus. The methods of land reclamation and fertilization will be examined with commentaries by authorities and examples of such applications in Indiana County. Emphasis will be given to the advantages and potential dangers of such practices.

From here the program will deal with the local controversy, its political ramifications, and the current status of sludge utilization in Indiana County. Included will be interviews with authorities on the subject. Local officials and residents opposing sludge utilization will be presented at a public hearing to better depict the scenario.

The program will end with statements from various parties involved and the narrator's restatement of the primary issues that the audience should consider in evaluating this issue.

The entire program will be designed to give the audience a basic understanding of the many aspects of this topic including the factual scientific and political controversies that have become involved. It will also pose the question of whether sludge utilization today may inflict severe penalties thus endangering the county's public health in the future.

REVIEW CHECKLIST

✓ A treatment is a basic script theme also known as a story-idea.

✓ You are to pick apart your idea and explain it in detail. A treatments is an important piece of scriptwriting work because it can be used in a way to display your idea prior to fully immersing yourself in an endeavor that might not be funded or published.

✓ You are to also explain your project in detail, with a specialized outline emphasizing drama and communicating excitement to the client.

✓ You are to also choose good words to keep the reader interested in your treatment.

✓ DO NOT use past tense, first person, and/or bullet points.

✓ The treatment must be written in a specific format if you want your project to receive fair consideration.

✓ You must write the treatment in third person.

QUESTIONS

1. What should you include in a treatment?
2. Why should you write treatments? Give examples.
3. Discuss the pros and cons of the treatment provided in this chapter.
4. Explain, in detail, what a good treatment is.

SAMPLE EXERCISE (Root)

"The Rivers Theory" is a short film based on the idea that no matter what decision you make, the same outcome is going to occur. The film starts with the main character, Chris Tjaden, entering his friend's apartment. He sits down at the kitchen table where his two best friends, Rylie and Spencer, are waiting to play poker. Chris tells them concerning news about his best friend, Jackson Rivers. Jackson and Chris are supposed to go on a hunting trip this upcoming weekend, when Jackson has a dream that he flipped his SUV on the way to the trip and dies. Jackson's dream frightened him so badly that he ended up canceling the hunting trip with Chris, and instead drives out East to see his girlfriend. The next morning, Chris sees the newspaper and on the front page is a headline that reads "Local Indiana Boy Dies in Tragic Car Wreck." Chris recognizes the picture as his best friend, Jackson Rivers, who had the dream that he had died.

Chris shows his friends the newspaper article and continues to tell them that he thinks it's more than coincidence that his best friend died the same way he had seen it in a dream. Chris begins to tell them about a theory that he thought of. He believes that there is a universal force that makes things happen no matter what decision people make. He uses the example that if he is supposed to break his leg that night, he's going to do it regardless of whether he's playing poker with them, or whether he is attacked by a lion. Either way he is going to break his leg, because that is what fate decided. Rylie and Spencer are sympathetic but tell Chris not to let the "theory" idea get to his head. Later that night, Chris goes home and does research the entire night about outcome theories and relates them to Jackson's death. Pretty soon the sun rises and Chris goes to work.

When Spencer sees Chris at work, he grows concerned because Chris looks exhausted. Chris accidently drops his briefcase and Spencer sees all of the research that Chris was doing the night before. During a break in their office meeting, Spencer calls Rylie and explains that he is concerned with Chris' state of mind because he thinks Chris is getting too wrapped up in his "theory." Rylie defends Chris, stating that they should cut him some slack since his best friend was just killed. Spencer agrees and hangs up. After work, Rylie calls Chris just to double-check that they were still on for their date that night. Chris yawns and replies that he will be there at 7 p.m.

Later that evening, Rylie is sitting at her kitchen table, with a meal prepared and candles lit. She looks at her phone which reads "7:41 p.m." She sighs, realizing that she has been stood up, and blows out the candles.

The next morning, Chris knocks on Rylie's door, wanting to apologize for falling asleep the night before and not being able to come over for dinner. Rylie gets upset and slams the door in Chris' face. Chris comes in anyway and argues that it was an accident and she was overreacting. Rylie argues that Chris fell asleep because he was up the previous night researching and that his theory was getting to his head. Chris agrees with Rylie and states that he'll burn all the research he had done on his theory about Jackson's death.

The next day, Chris burns his research as he said he would. That evening, he goes to a party with Rylie and Spencer. At the party, Chris isn't feeling well and ends up asking Rylie if she would be mad if he left and went home. Once Chris gets home, he turns on the television and is surprised by a breaking news story. The house that he was just partying at was on fire. Chris immediately calls Rylie to see if she and Spencer made it out safely. Rylie states that she and Spencer are fine, and asks if Chris is okay. Before he has time to respond, his smoke detector beings to beep, signaling that his house is on fire as well. Chris tells Rylie that he has to call her back. He immediately realizes that he was supposed to be in a fire regardless of whether or not he was at the party or at his house.

SAMPLE EXERCISE (Mason)

One Man's Trash Is Another Man's Art Supplies

In 1997 Charles J. Moore was on his way home across the Pacific Ocean, and he found a very large amount of debris floating in the water. We now know this large patch of trash as the Great Pacific Garbage patch. It has approximately 100 million tons of plastic in the water column. This floating patch is sucking nutrients from the ocean and poisoning the marine life that inhabits the area. There are multiple patches around the world because surface currents cause them when debris spins in a whirlpool effect.

The purpose of this documentary is to raise awareness of recycled materials congesting oceans and how individuals can make a difference. Indiana University of Pennsylvania's Art department is used as an example of how one group of students can make a difference.

Methodology that is pertinent to this documentary focuses on:

1. Addressing the problem
2. Breaking it down to its simplest form
3. Showing cause and effect of how it relates to the audience

4. Education on how to prevent the problem
5. Sustaining and recruiting on how to be a part of the cause

The program will first start at examining the issue on a very large scale and what it could do to the human population if overlooked. This will grab attention because when the audience looks at the present they will see how it can affect their children's children. After their attention is sustained with a very large topic, the key is to break it down and show how this one aspect of trash destroys marine life at its smallest stage. Then, moving through the marine food chain, each level is affected from the level previous to it.

The main point of how littering affects the ocean is the first point. This brings the audience to the second point: how it will affect them. Delving into areas on the globe where trash washing up on the beach is a constant problem that locals have to deal with shows the viewer that littering hurts people who don't even choose to litter. After the audience is educated on the world issue, the documentary steers them into the direction of how they can get involved.

An example of how the audience can get involved is when the documentary describes that this plastic can be utilized in many efficient and creative ways. It then dives in and describes the "One Island Project." An Art professor, Steve Loar, at Indiana University of Pennsylvania created the project. His personal quest to educate young artists into turning plastic refuse into beautiful pieces of artwork was implemented in his three-dimensional design class. Methods ranging from heat guns which melt and form plastic to metal rivets were used in the class, and he urged students to think outside of the box. He then asked his top students to accompany him on a trip where they would gather plastic on a beach setting and turn it into art. The trips ranged from the Bahamas to the rocky coasts of Scotland.

Describing the opportunity to students will interest them and they may want to join the group so they can make art on the beach. The film will then start the recruiting process and finally show some of the plastic works.

The program will end with visual imagery that shows how various plastics can be turned into beautiful and intricate pieces of artwork that can be sold to help fund the cause in eliminating trash from our ocean. It will strike home and educate the specialized audience of individuals because they can be a part of the program and make a difference in the small corner of Indiana, PA.

The entire program is designed to address the issue, educate, recruit, and finally sustain efforts. Recruitment is a key feature and if any information sticks with them the main effort is to put your trash in a receptacle because you never know where it will end up. Doing your part and individualizing the entire documentary forces the viewer to make personal changes in their life, and if ten viewers are effected by the documentary then that is ten people on the driving end of cleaning up the oceans.

EXERCISE

You are to write a treatment about a film idea of your choice. Make sure to review the criteria for writing a treatment and the actual example shown in this chapter. This assignment should be between two and five pages long.

9

MODIFIERS

"Preserve substance; modify form; know the difference." Dee Hock

LEARNING OBJECTIVES

By the end of the chapter, learners will be able to:

1. Explain what a modifiers is.
2. List a number of emotional modifiers.
3. Distinguish between a good and a great modifier.
4. Write scripts using modifiers.

QUICK DEBRIEF

In order to produce top-notch scripts, you need to understand the importance of applying modifiers of emotional impact and how they play a role in your story. Thinking about and using them should enable you to construct a script that could produce emotional impact.

WHAT IS A MODIFIER?

According to the *Merriam Dictionary*, a modifier is a person or a thing that makes partial or minor changes to something. A modifier in scriptwriting is no different. Samples of modifiers include

spatiotemporal, remoteness, humorous/serious, reality/fantasy, imita-
tion, and distortion. In this section and in the following section, I will
explain modifiers with examples.

EXAMPLE OF MODIFIERS APPLIED

There are several modifiers of emotional impact that have a tie to
scriptwriting. I will discuss them in the lines below.

- **Spatial remoteness, measured in proximity.** Near objects have a
  stronger emotional impact than objects far away. Think about
  this for a second or two and tie your thoughts to the work of
  Alfred Hitchcock and his "Psycho" movie scene. The woman's
  close-up face proximity to screen produces an emotional impact
  on the audience. A far away scene would not have as much of
  an impact. This is because the closer the scene, the more emotional impact it will have on the audience.
- **Temporal remoteness, measured in proximity.** Events that are
  happening now have far more impact than events that happened
  long ago. Today is September 17th, 2011, and we are seeing one
  of the worst floods in Pennsylvania history. Today, the emotional
  impacts of this natural disaster are affecting us quite significantly.
  Whenever this flood event becomes a "thing of the past," residents of Pennsylvania won't "feel" as much as we feel today.
- **Humorous/Serious.** Serious scenes often have more emotional
  impact than humorous ones, even though in some instances,
  humorous events can also have a strong emotional impact, like
  in the case of "Easy Rider" in the '60s when a couple was shot
  in the movie and the audience laughed to release the emotion.
  However, more often than not, serious scenes often provide
  more emotional impact.
- **Reality/Fantasy.** Reality has more emotional impact than fantasy. This might be why we have seen an explosion of reality
  TV series in the last decade in the United States. When you see

a scene of blood in a movie, for example "The Passion of the Christ," it has a stronger emotional impact than seeing a cartoon's blood in South Park. The more real the image, the more impact it will have.

- **Identification.** These terms have an impact on one's emotion and should be taken into account when it comes to scriptwriting. One of the classic examples of identification is with the actor Charles Bronson. In his movies, somebody is killed and violence is associated with this act, and we identify Charles Bronson to be there and do justice, making the audience identify with him as a "justice character."

- **Distortion/bias/stereotype.** These are also modifiers of emotional impact. The more distortion, bias, and stereotype, the more emotional impact the audience will have. In the movie *Lean on Me,* Morgan Freeman plays the role of a tough principal in an inner city school. His distorted view of his own faculty can also be seen as a modifier of emotional impact.

- **Consequences in human terms.** There are two types of human consequences, physical and emotional. The more physical the consequences, the more the emotional impact the audience will experience. In the film "Rocky" Sylvester Stallone plays the role of an aspiring boxing champion who is beaten over and over again. The actual blood marks on his face were physical consequences of punches which resulted in strong emotional impact in the audience. In fact, the scene in which he screams, "Adrian!" is an example of that.

  Emotional human consequences also play an impact in scriptwriting. In the film "Radio" the audience sees an example of how mental retardation affects the emotions of others. The worse the emotional consequences, the stronger the overall emotional impact on a particular audience.

- **Inappropriate sexuality/obscenity.** The more sex and obscenity, the stronger the emotional impact an audience will experience. In the movie "Orange Mechanic" this concept was applied as the director mixed both nudity scenes as well as obscenities. In addition to that, he used concepts of violence which made the movie quite "grotesque" to the eyes of most viewers, yet making it a hit in 1980s.

- **Slow motion/stop action.** Contrary to what you might think, stop action has a stronger emotional impact than slow motion. Alfred Hitchcock was a master when it came to stop actions. Stop and think about the movie "Psycho." The camera stops! The last scene in "Sweet November" is another example of how a camera stop has an impact on the audience. One can deduce that she committed suicide on the bridge in the last scene of the movie.

REVIEW CHECKLIST

✓ Near objects have a stronger emotional impact than objects far away.

✓ In order to produce top-notch scripts, you need to understand the importance of applying modifiers of emotional impact and how they play a role in your story.

✓ The more distortion, bias, and stereotype, the more emotional impact the audience will have.

✓ Reality has more emotional impact than fantasy.

✓ Stop action has a stronger emotional impact than slow motion.

✓ One's emotion should be taken into account when it comes to scriptwriting.

✓ A modifier is a person or a thing that makes partial or minor changes to something.

QUESTIONS

1. What are the different types of modifiers?
2. Why should you review the modifiers prior to writing your script?
3. How many modifiers should you have in a script?
4. What is the difference between a good and not so good modifier?

SAMPLE EXERCISE (Ranish)

Spatial Remoteness, Measured in Proximity: Objects closer to the screen have more of an emotional impact than those further away. In the opening scene of the movie "Scream 2," a woman is in a movie theater watching a movie of the infamous murderer in a mask. All around her are people dressed as the killer. During a particular gruesome scene in the movie, everyone jumps up with their fake knives and pretends to stab other people. The man next to the main woman jumps up and starts stabbing her. The camera jumps from close-ups of the man stabbing her, to close-ups of the woman's face. This is very impactful because of all the emotion that can be seen on her face.

Temporal Remoteness, Measured in Proximity: Events that are happening now have more impact than events that happened long ago. The movie "The Messenger," is about soldiers who have to deliver the news to families that their children died during the war in Iraq. This has a lot of impact because the war is still fresh in our minds, and a lot of people can relate to losing children in the war or losing a child in a different situation.

Humorous/Serious: Serious scenes have more emotional impact than humorous scenes. The movie "Home Room" is about a school shooting. It is a very serious movie. At one point in the film, all of the survivors get together to talk about what happened and how affected they were by it. It is a very emotional scene because it is very serious.

Reality/Fantasy: Reality has more of an emotional impact than fantasy. The documentary film "The Horse Boy," is about an autistic boy whose dedicated parents travel to Mongolia to find treatment for their son through horseback riding. The reason it is so moving is because you actually get to see the heartbreak on the parents' face. It is a documentary about real life, and that it why it is so emotional.

Identification: Identification is when the audience identifies and roots for the character. In the movie "The Lovely Bones," the audience can identify with the grieving father and sister of the murdered girl. We, the audience, want justice for the murdered girl, and we want closure for her family. This is what gives it such an emotional impact, because we can identify with the characters.

Distortion/Bias/Stereotype: The more distortion, bias, and stereotype, the more emotional impact the audience will have. The movie "There's Something about Mary" is a comedy, but it still has emotional impact because of the character of Warren. He is Mary's mentally handicapped brother. He is big and goofy and innocent. Because of all of these qualities, it is easy to feel for him and sympathize for him.

Consequences in Human Terms: Emotional and physical consequences in humans add emotional impact. In the movie "Million Dollar Baby," Hilary Swank's character tries to become a professional boxer. In one scene Hilary Swank is in the boxing ring and her opponent punches her after the match is over and breaks her neck. As she is falling, everything is in slow motion and you can really see the physical impact.

Inappropriate Sexuality/Obscenity: The more sex and obscenity, the stronger the emotional impact is. In the movie "28 Days," Sandra Bullock plays an alcoholic in rehab. While she is there she meets an alcoholic and sex addict and there is a lot of tension between them. In one scene, when they are both very vulnerable, they have a sexual interaction that is very intense.

Slow Motion/Stop Action: Stop action has more impact than slow motion. In the television show "NCIS," a series of photographs (just like stop-motion), is used to show glimpses of the crime and what will happen. This has a lot of impact because the mind is left to fill in the blanks.

Spatial Remoteness, Measured in Proximity: Again, objects closer to the screen have more of an emotional impact than those further away. In the movie "Anywhere But Here," Natalie Portman's character loses someone close to her. When she goes to his funeral, the camera pans across all of the sad faces in the audience crying, and then the camera stops on Natalie's face. The close-up of Natalie is very emotional because you can see how upset she is. This would not be as emotional if it was shot from further away.

EXERCISE

You are to go online or to the library, select ten movies, find at least ten modifiers of emotional impact along with the scenes and write it down in this exercise as a narrative. Do your very best.

10

RADIO PSA

"Radio PSA is like TV, informative and fun."   Unknown writer

LEARNING OBJECTIVES

By the end of the chapter, learners will be able to:

1. Write effective community calendars.
2. Differentiate between good and bad radio PSAs.
3. List three radio PSA tips.
4. Explain radio PSA format to media professionals.

HOW USEFUL IS IT?

Radio Public Service Announcements (PSAs) are very important even though writing TV scripts is often seen as the main focal point in scriptwriting. In public radio stations for example, PSAs play a role in the overall operation of the radio station. When I delivered the Dr. A show at WIUP FM, I read a number of community calendars and single radio PSAs in between songs and station IDs. Depending on the mission statement of the station, radio PSAs could be an important component of the radio station, making it quite useful.

FORMAT

Community calendars can be produced using the following format. It starts with the word "Community Calendar" at the top of the page. You are to then write "START DATE:" (In Caps) followed by the work Immediate (Low Caps) making it, START DATE: Immediate. After the START DATE, you are to write "KILL DATE:" followed by the day of the week, month of the year, day of the month, and hour of the day, e.g., Thursday, September 22, 7PM, making it KILL DATE: Thursday, September 22, 7PM. After KILL DATE, you are to write the word READ (In Caps) with the following format, –READ–. The body of your message is to be written in all caps and double spaced followed by the term –END– after your message.

Writing Radio PSAs is one of the simplest formats in scriptwriting. All you have to do is write your PSA with words that the radio host can read with ease, make the document in all caps, and double space. Radio PSAs are used extensively and are a required component in college radio stations.

Radio PSAs can also have other formats. Sometimes, scriptwriters use the word V.O. (Voice over) on the left column of the script to indicate that there is a voice over.

RADIO PSA TIPS

There are a large number of tips when it comes to writing radio PSAs. I will share a few with you in this chapter. Let's get started!

- **Don't be repetitive.** Being repetitive is a waste of air time SO, don't do it.
- **Don't use clichés.** Clichés are distracting and can void the meaning of your messages. When clichés are used, listeners tend to stop paying attention to your message.
- **Cut the crap. Tell only the necessary.** Radio PSA is supposed to be concise, to the point. Radio, different from newspapers, is

not a medium to write extensively. Writing too much bores the listeners.

- **Use dashes when writing acronyms.** Every time you write an acronym, such as IUP, you are to write, I-U-P.
- **If you can use three why ten?** If you can tell the story with three words, don't use ten! If you can tell the story with fewer words, do it!
- **Use present tense always.** In radio, you are to write in present tense.
- **Write in speaking style.** In radio you are to write conversationally. Write as if you are telling a story to your friend.
- **Approximate numbers.** Rather than writing, "I have 295 golf balls," you should write, "I have nearly 300 golf balls."
- **If one-to-ten, write them out.** If you are writing numbers one to ten, make sure you write them out.
- **Avoid disclosure of age.** Unless you are instructed to read about a criminal on air by the police, avoid disclosure of age.
- **Avoid third person.** If you have to mention somebody else's name, use it. AVOID he/she in your radio scripts.
- **Flow and short sentences.** In radio scriptwriting, you are to write scripts that have flow and short sentences.
- **Avoid gossip.** If you are not sure, don't advertise!

REVIEW CHECKLIST

- ✓ Avoid third person in your radio scripts.
- ✓ PSAs play a role in the overall operation of the radio station.
- ✓ You are to write scripts that have flow and short sentences.
- ✓ You are to write in present tense.
- ✓ Writing Radio PSAs is one of the simplest formats in scriptwriting.
- ✓ You are to write conversationally.
- ✓ Being repetitive is a waste of air time.

QUESTIONS

1. Why shouldn't you be repetitive when writing Radio PSAs?
2. What is the difference between a community calendar and a radio PSA?
3. If you are to describe what a PSA is to a friend, how would you describe it?
4. Write everything you know about radio PSAs.

SAMPLE EXERCISE (McClelland)

START DATE: Immediate
KILL DATE: December 20, 2012

–READ–

SAINT MARY'S CHURCH IS HOLDING A TOYS FOR TOTS DRIVE. TOYS FOR TOTS IS WHERE PEOPLE BRING IN TOYS AND THEY GO OUT TO CHILDREN WHO WON'T HAVE ANYTHING ON CHRISTMAS DAY. THE TOYS FOR TOTS FOUNDATION REACHES AROUND 1,000 CHILDREN IN THE WEST PENNSYLVANIA AREA. ANY DONATIONS TO SAINT MARY'S CHURCH ARE GREATLY APPRECIATED AND WILL MAKE A CHILD SMILE ON CHRISTMAS DAY. FOR MORE INFORMATION ON THE TOYS FOR TOTS DRIVE, CHECK YOUR LOCAL NEWSPAPER OR CALL SAINT MARY'S CHURCH AT 724-242-3849.

–END–

EXERCISE

Write three Radio PSAs following the criteria presented in this chapter. Format is key for this assignment. Good luck.

11

FEATURES

"A lot of feature films do two pages a day."   Timothy Bottoms

LEARNING OBJECTIVES

By the end of the chapter, learners will be able to:

1. Write well planned feature stories.
2. Understand its format.
3. Name an outlet where a feature story might be aired.
4. Explain what a feature story is.

INTRODUCTION

Features are a common type of production, often aired in public outlets like National Public Radio (NPR) or in local television stations. Features are often assigned to media professionals to report about important events and are often political or sociological. It is not uncommon for feature stories to start by introducing background information to tell what the story is about in order to provide a frame of reference to the audience. It is important for you to write about people and/or problems and events that carry community interest.

FORMAT

Feature stories must have a title in all caps with the word feature in it. It should also have the name of the author below also in all caps. After these components are fulfilled, a host introduction must follow, in all caps (Hyde, 2002).

SIDNEY CROSBY LEFT THE PITTSBURGH PIRATES FEATURE

LUIS ALMEIDA

HOST INTRO: HOCKEY PLAYER SYDNEY CROSBY, ONE OF PITTSBURGH PENGUINS' ALL-TIME STARS, WILL BE MOVING TO THE TORONTO MAPLE LEAFS IN THE END OF THE 2013 SEASON. THE CAPTAIN OF THE PENGUINS AND HOCKEY SUPERSTAR WILL LEAVE BEHIND MILLIONS OF FANS TO FIND A NEW HOME BACK IN CANADA AND A SALARY THREE TIMES LARGER. FRANCHISE MANAGER JOHN SMITH WAS DETERMINED TO BRING CROSBY BACK TO CANADA DUE TO PATRIOTIC AND SKILLS REASONS. LUIS ALMEIDA HAS THIS REPORT LIVE FROM ONTARIO, CANADA.

Although a sound effect and a description of the sound effect might not be present in all feature stories, it is often used after the host introduction. Make sure to make the sound effect and its description are in all caps.

SFX: CANADIAN NATIONAL ANTHEM PLAYS.

After the sound effect, you can then write what the main character/ reporter will talk about. Make sure also that the name of the reporter is in all caps but what they say is not.

LUIS: Hockey player Sidney Crosby is the youngest hockey player in history to win the Stanley cup. Although Crosby's career with the Penguins was already in turmoil due to an injury that has been impeding him to play again, an effort from patriotic Canadians sealed the deal. The initiative was lead by John Smith, General Manager of the Toronto Maple Leafs and a few Crosby high school friends. The "Crosby back to Canada" initiative is a hit in his hometown in Canada.

You might want to include another sound effect after the main character and before the actualities. Comments given by third parties are a good idea as they give feelings to a story. Make sure to use all caps for actualities also and if transitions are included, they should be in parenthesis.

SFX #2: TOWN PEOPLE SCREAMING "CROSBY! CROSBY!"

ACTUALITY #1 (JACK BLACK) SIDNEY BELONGS TO CANADA AND OUR COMMUNITY. WE NEED HIM BACK. I CAN'T BELIEVE THAT WE WERE BUDDIES IN HIGH SCHOOL, MAN.

ACTUALITY #2 (JANE BROWN) WE MISS HIM. OUR COMMUNITY AND NATION NEED CROSBY BACK. SINCE HIS DEPARTURE TO PITTSBURGH, WE HAVE MISSED HIM. HIS DAILY STOP IN OUR BAKERY CAN'T BE FORGOTTEN.

After two actualities, you might want to have either a sound effect or the main character back. In here, I will bring a sound effect and then the character to end the feature.

SFX #3: VOICE OF THE GENERAL MANAGER SAYING "CROSBY IS OURS."

LUIS: CANADA IS READY TO EMBRACE CROSBY BACK. HIS TOWN FRIENDS AND TORONTO MAPLE LEAFS' GENERAL MANAGER ARE WAITING FOR HIM DILIGENTLY. I DON'T BLAME THEM. FOR NPR, I AM LUIS ALMEIDA. I WILL SEE YOU GUYS NEXT TIME.

REVIEW CHECKLIST

✓ You might want to include another sound effect after the main character and before the actualities.

✓ After two actualities, you might want to have either a sound effect or the main character.

✓ If transitions are included, they should be in parenthesis.

✓ Make sure also that the name of the reporter is in all caps but what they say is not.

✓ Feature stories must have a title in all caps with the word feature in it.

✓ Features are a common type of production, often aired in public outlets like NPR or in local television stations.

✓ Features are often assigned to media professionals to report about important events and may be political or sociological.

QUESTIONS

1. What is an actuality? Write three sample actualities.
2. Why are feature stories so popular? Which outlets would broadcast such stories?
3. Should you develop feature stories for all occasions? Yes? No?
4. Give an example of a political feature story idea.

SAMPLE EXERCISE (Ranish)

HOST INTRO: AFTER COMING BACK FROM A 0–3 DEFICIT, THE PITTSBURGH PENGUINS ARE READY TO TAKE ON THE PHILADELPHIA FLYERS IN GAME 7 OF THE SERIES. THIS SERIES HAS BEEN EXTREMELY STRENUOUS FOR BOTH TEAMS. NOT ONLY HAVE THE TEAMS BEEN PUTTING UP A FIGHT, BUT THE FANS HAVE BEEN HEATED AS WELL.

SFX: CROWD CHANTING, CHEERING, AND WHISTLING.

SALLY ALBRIGHT: The start of the series promised a much different outcome for the Philadelphia Flyers. Taking a commanding 3-0 lead, the Flyers and the fans expected to have this one in the bag. However, the Pittsburgh Penguins would not give up. In game 4 of the Stanley Cup Playoffs, the Penguins, on the brink of elimination, came back to win with a final score of 5-4. The Penguins came back without their prominent scorer, James Neal. Games 5 and 6 followed the same hard-hitting and high intensity format of the rest of the series, with the Penguins pulling off the nearly impossible and staying in the cup race. Now on the evening of game 7, the player and fans of both teams are ready for the most important game yet.

SFX #2:   MIXED CHANTS OF "LET'S GO PENGUINS!" AND "LET'S GO FLYERS!"

ACTUALITY #1 (PENS FAN):   THE PENS HAVE COME THIS FAR AND THEY AREN'T GOING TO GIVE UP NOW! THEY'VE GOT NOTHING TO LOSE AND IT'S TIME TO PUT THE FLYERS WHERE THEY BELONG!

ACTUALITY #2 (FLYERS FAN):   THE PENS MAY HAVE COME BACK TO EVEN UP THE SERIES BUT NO WAY WILL OUR BOYS LETS THEM WIN THIS GAME! THIS IS OUR YEAR TO WIN THE CUP, AND THE PENGUINS WON'T STAND IN OUR WAY!

SFX #3:   MORE CROWDS CHEERING AND ARGUING BETWEEN FANS.

SALLY ALBRIGHT: Not only are the fans heated, the players aren't exactly playing nice either. Both teams haven't been shy about their feelings for one another.

SFX #4: SOUNDS OF REPORTERS TALKING AND LOCKER ROOM SOUNDS.

ACTUALITY #3 (SIDNEY CROSBY): I THINK IT'S PRETTY OBVIOUS THAT WE DON'T PARTICULARLY LIKE THEM AND THEY DON'T LIKE US. THIS SERIES HAS BEEN ONE OF THE TOUGHEST WE'VE EVER FACED AND IT'S ONLY ROUND 1, BUT WE HAVE TO PUT EVERYTHING THAT HAS HAPPENED IN THE PAST AND FOCUS ON THIS ONE GAME.

ACTUALITY #4 (CLAUDE GIROUX): OF COURSE IT'S NO SECRET THE PENS AND THE FLYERS DON'T GET ALONG AND HAVEN'T GOTTEN ALONG FOR YEARS. THIS SERIES HAS PROVED THAT, AND IT ALL COMES DOWN TO THIS ONE GAME TO SEE WHO THE TRULY BETTER TEAM IS.

SALLY ALBRIGHT: Amongst all the bad blood between the two hockey clubs, former Penguins' superstar turned Flyer fan, Jamior Jagr has been very vocal as well.

ACTUALITY #5 (JAMIOR JAGR): THERE WILL ALWAYS BE A SPECIAL PLACE IN MY HEART FOR THE PITTSBURGH PENGUINS, BUT MY FOCUS IS ON THE FLYERS NOW. MY GOAL IS TO GET US A CUP, AND I WON'T STOP UNTIL I REACH THAT GOAL.

SFX #5: OUTRO MUSIC TO END SHOW SOFT IN BACKGROUND.

SALLY ALBRIGHT: Well, this game will certainly be one for the books. Be sure to tune in tonight at 7:30 pm to see who will win in this keystone clash. Until next time, I'm Sally Albright.

EXERCISE

You are to write a political feature story of your choice including a host, four sound effects, and five actualities. Make sure to end with the host. Good luck.

12

RADIO DRAMA FORMAT

"Acted drama requires surrender of one's self, sympathetic absorption in the play as it develops." George Baker

LEARNING OBJECTIVES

By the end of the chapter, learners will be able to:

1. Write a radio drama.
2. Identify key elements of a great radio drama.
3. Discuss whether radio dramas are dead or alive.
4. Name three criteria that make great radio dramas.

IS IT STILL SEXY?

No question. You will quickly realize that radio dramas are not as sexy as they once were. However, it does not mean we shouldn't produce them! Radio dramas lost their shine in the '50s after the introduction of television. However, creating a piece that brings listeners to a story with a struggle resolution format and providing a plot with elements of surprise can and probably should impact any audience at any period in time. People often enjoy dialogues with appropriate atmospheres where they feel emotion, as long as you have a purpose.

When I was in college, I heard the comment, "Radio is a dead medium" until I listened to Howard Stern and satellite radio. I would not be surprised to see radio dramas (good ones) coming back again, due to the long commute Americans are now facing in their professions. I believe . . . I believe in radio dramas. They are here to stay. Are you ready for the challenge? Just make sure to be clear with your language and be precise.

RADIO DRAMA FORMAT

Radio drama format is one of the easiest formats in the industry. Garvey and Rivers (1982, p. 39.) provide a great format for us to use in this section. We could make this section much longer but why make this complicated if we can simplify? So, let's get started.

- You are to use the name of each speaker an inch from the left edge of the page.
- You are to use capital letters and put a colon after the names.
- You are to indent all dialogs two inches from the left edge of the page.
- You are to set the right margin an inch from the right edge of the page.
- Music and sound effect cues go one inch from the left edge of the page in underlined capitals.
- You are to type dialog with regular upper- and lower-case letters.
- Type all directions in capital letters.
- Put short directions in parenthesis inside the dialog.
- Start longer directions one inch from the left edge of the page, running to one inch from the right edge without parenthesis.
- Copies for radio are often singled space.
- If the script is longer than one page, break the script one inch from the bottom of the page, double space and type "(More)" centered. In the next page, repeat the name of the speaker and type "(CONT'D)" under the name.

REVIEW CHECKLIST

✓ Copies for radio are often single spaced.

✓ Radio drama format is one of the easiest formats in the industry.

✓ Put short directions in parentheses inside the dialog.

✓ Radio dramas lost their shine in the '50s after the introduction of television.

✓ Type all directions in capital letters.

✓ You are to use capital letters and put a colon after the names.

✓ You are to type dialog with regular upper- and lower-case letters.

QUESTIONS

1. Name five elements you could use in a radio drama format.
2. What would you do to bring radio dramas back into the market?
3. Why should you invest time and money in radio dramas?
4. Can you tell directions in lower cap letters? Justify your response.

SAMPLE EXERCISE (MASON)

NARRATOR: Good evening ladies and gentlemen and welcome to another weekly edition of your favorite who done it drama: Ah Ha! Tonight we find ourselves in the old McAdams mansion just outside of a small suburban town in Pennsylvania. The estate has been abandoned for years after the murder of Mr. McAdams. The place is notoriously haunted and strange occurrences keep happening whenever unwanted strangers come crawling to investigate. A group of teenagers decide to tempt fate and take their chances inside the mansion for a night. Little do they know that not everyone would leave with their lives. We enter the scene as Gary, Joe, Sam, Ashley, Jenna, and Vern are wandering around the place looking for anything ominous or creepy, but they have come up empty so far.

SAM: Listen guys this is really starting to become a waste of my time. All I see is a poorly decorated house with some broken mirrors and dusty furniture. I could be at home playing video games right now. If we don't see anything in the next five minutes I'm ditching this place and getting my Super Mario on.

GARY: Yeah who's idea was this anyway? I don't even believe in ghosts. I mean, they're just spirits right? How is some transparent supernatural being going to physically harm me? I think old man McAdams is in a box six feet under and isn't going to show up tonight. Let's just go home.

SFX: *DOOR SLAMS SHUT IN THE DISTANCE*

VERN: What the hell was that? Wait where's Ashley?

SFX: *THREE LOUD THUDS COME FROM THE CEILING*

ASHLEY: Aaaaahhhhhhh!

THE GROUP SPRINTS UP THE STAIRS TO CHECK ON ASHLEY, BUT THE ROOM SHE IS IN IS LOCKED. AFTER SEVERAL FAILED ATTEMPTS AT OPENING THE DOOR, VERN GETS A RUNNING START AND BREAKS THE DOOR OFF OF ITS HINGES.

VERN: Oh my god! Ashley!

NARRATOR: The group of teens stares at the horror before their eyes. Ashley has been brutally murdered with an apparent knife wound to the chest. There is blood everywhere, indicating that there was a struggle. There is a message written in her blood that spells out "YOU ARE NOT WELCOME HERE." The teens are frozen in shock, unable to process the sight in front of them. The catatonic stares are broken by a loud crack of thunder and flash of lightning coming from outside.

SFX: *CRRACK!*

JENNA: Jesus Christ! I knew we shouldn't have come here! What are we going to do now? Who would do such a thing? If we call the police they are going to think one of us did it.

GARY: Maybe one of us did . . .

VERN: What the hell are you trying to say here Gary? Do you think this is some kind of sick joke? Ashley's dead and we were all downstairs when we heard the scream, so there's no way any of us could have done it.

JOE: Not everyone . . .

VERN: Who wasn't down there then?

JOE: Well, Jenna wasn't in sight when we were talking about how lame this place was, and if I remember correctly Jenna, didn't Ashley's father fire yours from the steel mill last week?

THE GROUP SLOWLY TURNS THEIR HEAD AROUND TO JENNA TO LOOK FOR SOME SORT OF JUSTIFICATION. JENNA IS NOW SWEATING BADLY AND APPEARS ANXIOUS AS SHE SLOWLY STARTS BACKING TOWARDS THE DOOR.

JENNA: Oh no, you guys are not going to put this on me! I didn't do anything wrong! My Dad was just an honest man trying to make a living, but I guess stock points are worth more to Ashley's dad than my father's career. Either way, I would never do anything to Ashley! Did you all forget that we were best friends?

JOE: Then where were you when we were downstairs?

JENNA: I was . . . I was . . .

GARY: That's it I'm calling the cops. Vern hold her down till they get here.

JENNA: NO! I was looking for extra food in the house, alright? Happy now? Money was pretty tight at our house before my dad was fired and now my family doesn't even have enough food to feed our family. I was looking for some cans or something to bring back for my little brothers.

GARY: You still have the motive though and weren't there when we heard the screams. I'm not convinced. Vern . . .

JENNA:　You gotta believe me! Look at my hands! There's no blood on them. How could I have written that message and washed it off in time to be back with you guys when you tried to get in the door?

SFX:　SHATTERING GLASS COMING FROM DOWNSTAIRS

VERN:　What was that?

JOE:　Quick let's go!

THE GANG RUSHES DOWN THE STAIRS IN A FRENZY, AND JOE LEADING THE PACK TRIPS ON A CREAKY STEP AND THEY ALL FALL TO THE BOTTOM OF THE STAIRCASE.

SFX:　LOUD SOUNDS OF PEOPLE BANGING OFF THE RICKETY STAIRCASE

JENNA:　Joe you idiot!

JOE:　It wasn't my fault; it is this stupid house and the stupid stairs and let's just get out of here!

SFX:　THE SOUND OF A TV FILLS THE SILENCE AFTER THE FALL

NARRATOR:　After Joe gets up and starts walking to the ballroom he sees something that looks very out of place. A large flat screen is on and the picture is very fuzzy. They enter into the room and they all start freaking out because there is Sam sitting on the floor with a Nintendo 64 controller wrapped around his neck. Jenna rushes in to see if she can revive him but there is no hope; he is already gone. As they watch the TV a message appears and reads, "Get out while you still can."

VERN:　Oh my God why is this HAPPENING! Yeah let's get the hell out of here!

JOE:　Ok!

JENNA:　I don't want to die!

JOE:　Hey Vern why are you touching my neck?

VERN: Bro I'm not touching your neck.

SFX: THE DOOR SLAMS AND THE DEADBOLT LATCHES SHUT

JENNA: I wanna go home! I wanna go home!

JENNA IS A MESS AND IS BAWLING HER EYES OUT

VERN: Well I don't think that's going to happen . . . .

VERN SMILING AT JOE

JOE: Yeah Jenna you won't be going home anytime soon. You really pissed us both off when you turned both of us down to the prom. I mean Vern had no shot anyway but you turned me down and nobody turns Joey T. down.

JENNA: Joey I am so sorry just please don't kill me.

VERN: Let's have him come in first Joe.

JOE: Sounds like a good idea, come on in Uncle McAdams!

SFX: THE DOOR UNLATCHES AND SWINGS OPEN

JENNA: AHHH! NOO!

THEY OPEN THE DOOR JUST AS JENNA STARTS SCREAMING.

JENNA: You guys!!!!!!!!

EVERYONE: Got ya!

TO JENNA'S DISMAY SHE WAS ON HIGH SCHOOL PUNKED. EVERYTHING WAS A SETUP AND SHE WAS PRANKED! SEE YOU NEXT TIME ON "AH HAH"!

JOE: Thanks for all of the help from our friends at MTV. We could not have done it without you. Wexford Seniors rock!!

NARRATOR: We will see you next time on another frightening story of "Ah Ha!"

EXERCISE

Write a radio drama, including a narrator, two characters, a plot, elements of surprise, a dialog with a purpose, and an element of suspense. Also, make sure to include sound effects and other extras.

13

SOUND PORTRAITS

"Sound portraits are my favorite feature story writing." Luis Almeida

LEARNING OBJECTIVES

By the end of the chapter, learners will be able to:

1. Write effective sound portraits.
2. Explain what sound portraits are.
3. Deconstruct sound portraits.
4. Tell when to use sound portraits.

INTRODUCTION

Sound portraits are also types of feature stories, with the distinction that they only have actualities in the script. Sound portraits are made of third party statements without any form of commentary. One of the advantages of this type of feature story is its price and fast pace of production. This type of scriptwriting is often short and introduced by an announcer (Hyde, 2003).

FORMAT

Sound portraits start with a title in all caps, followed by the title in lower caps and the name of the media professional.

IUP ALUMNI
A Sound Portrait by Luis Almeida

After the title, you will need to write what the announcer is going to say about your sound portrait. The announcer's tag will be in all caps. Its content should be in lower caps.

ANNCR: Several IUP alumni will be returning to town for homecoming. Alumni from the '50s, '60s, '70s, and '80s will be attending the celebration on campus and in its surroundings. The homecoming queen and king will be leading the festivities along with the town's mayor. This event has the potential to be one of the greatest homecoming celebrations in the history of IUP due to its size. From Indiana, Pennsylvania, Luis Almeida has the details of this Alumni event.

After finishing with the announcer's introduction, some special effects could give a better feeling to this story prior to bringing the actualities. Special effects are a vital part of a well constructed sound portrait. Special effects should be in all caps as well as its contents.

SFX: IUP MARCHING BAND PLAYING FIGHT SONG.

SFX: GO IUP!

After the announcer and a couple of sound effects, it is time to bring the actualities. You will need to write the name of the actualities in all caps but the content in lower caps. See the example below.

JOHN: Today is IUP's day. Our university has years of excellence and deserves this day. I am a proud IUP alumnus and am glad to be here. How can anybody not attend this institution?

MARK: My name is Mark Johns. I attended IUP in the late '80s as a student of communications. I love this school and will always love it. Why? Because attending IUP was the very best four years of my life.

In this type of scriptwriting, it is not abnormal to have over a dozen actualities. It is also not abnormal to have music in addition to sound effects. Music must be in all caps and its description in lower caps.

MUSIC: IUP Alma Mater playing.

SFX: CROWD CLAPPING, FADE OUT.

Although you don't have to finish a sound portrait this way, I would recommend that you do, especially if you are new to scriptwriting. End a sound portrait with an announcer's note, like the one written below.

ANNCR: Luis Almeida, live, from Indiana, PA.

REVIEW CHECKLIST

- ✓ You will need to write the name of the actualities in all caps but the content in lower caps.
- ✓ One of the advantages of this type of feature story is its price and fast pace of production.
- ✓ This type of scriptwriting is often short and introduced by an announcer.
- ✓ Music must be in all caps and its description in lower caps.
- ✓ In this type of scriptwriting, it is not abnormal to have over a dozen actualities.
- ✓ Sound portraits are also types of feature stories, with the distinction that they only have actualities in the script.
- ✓ Sound portraits start with a title in all caps, followed by the title in lower caps and the name of the media professional.

QUESTIONS

1. What are actualities? Explain in detail.
2. When are sound portraits used? Explain when sound portraits should and should not be used.
3. If you were a freelancer, how would you market yourself to sell sound portraits?
4. Go online and analyze a sound portrait and tell your group what you have found.

SAMPLE EXERCISE (Mason)

WHAT'S NEXT FOR THE PITTSBURGH PENGUINS?
A Sound Portrait by Ryan and Chris

ANNCR: In a scenario that may seem a little unfamiliar to most Pittsburgh fans, the Penguins find themselves in a three game hole against the Philadelphia Flyers. While a five year championship drought wouldn't be embarrassing to most teams around the league, a perennial powerhouse like the Penguins expect nothing but a Stanley Cup every season. But now Pittsburgh is staring a four game winning streak in the face after another tough loss Wednesday and has to examine what exactly went wrong and where they can improve as a team.

SFX: PITTSBURGH ROOT SPORTS THEME SONG, AND THEN FADE OUT TO ACTUALITIES

DAVE: We love the Pens. It was a tough loss but they need to get this one out of their head and start playing like a team again.

SUE: This is going to be a tough series and I don't know if they are going to make it from the way they have been playing.

RICH: Somebody needs to teach Scotty Hartnell a lesson and I know Orpik is our man to do the job.

CHRIS: I know that we can get through this. We are the Penguins and we always come out on top.

AMANDA: I have flyer fans at my work and they are so annoying, so I have been wearing my Lemieux jersey to work every game we have. Let's do this Pens!

TYLER: Now that Crosby has been back for a while we are unstoppable! The past games have been all flukes and we are going to win this series.

RYAN: Philadelphia may doubt us now but we have just been getting warmed up. We are going all the way this year to bring the cup back to the Burgh!

BRITTANY: The Pens really blew this last game and their passing was just terribly off. They need to do some more shooting drills and get their passes off faster.

JEN: Fleury really needs to start staying in the net. I don't know if I could watch another game because he gets me so nervous.

TONY: LETS GOOOOOOOOOO PENS, show the Phil-tha-delphia Flyers what we are made of and send them back to the other side of the state!

ANNCR: If there's one thing we've learned after these first three games, it is that Penguins fans are as resilient as they come. There's no swaying their opinion and the belief that the Penguins are going to come back and take this series is almost unanimous. If there's one team that has the talent, ability, and will to win, it's your Pittsburgh Penguins. For Chris Mason, I'm Ryan Brown live from Pittsburgh, PA.

MUSIC: Root Sports theme song plays.

SFX: GOAL HORN GOING OFF, FADE OUT.

EXERCISE

Write a sound portrait using the following elements—Two announcers (ANNCR), two special effects (SFX), ten actualities, and two music (MUSIC). Use your creativity and the format included in this chapter.

14

TWO COLUMN
FEATURE STORY

"Do you know what I'm working on now? My first feature as a director." Faye Dunaway

LEARNING OBJECTIVES

By the end of the chapter, learners will be able to:

1. Write two column feature stories.
2. Examine two column feature stories.
3. List the elements contained in the two column format.
4. Analyze two column scripts.

INTRODUCTION

A two column feature story is often the preferred format for TV scriptwriting. Camera shots, object and scene descriptions, video and audio columns, fadeouts, characters, and an array of creativity makes this scriptwriting format a necessity, if you wish to write scripts professionally (Hyde, 2003). I decided to leave this format last due to its importance in the field. As an educator and Instructional Designer, I have found that most students learn the most from what is introduced in the beginning and the end instruction. Guess what? This is the end! I really want you to remember this format! Let's get started.

FORMAT

A two column feature story can be more detailed than a single column feature story. You should start the script with a title in all caps and the word reporter (also in all caps) followed by a colon and the name of the reporter in lower caps.

SYDNEY CROSBY GOES BACK HOME

REPORTER: Luis Almeida

After that, you should divide the page with video on the left and audio on the right. Both words all caps.

VIDEO	AUDIO

All video text is to be in all caps. Camera shots can also be put under the video column in all caps. Sounds are to be displayed under the audio column in all caps. Reporter voice is to be written in low caps with the name of the reporter in all caps. Third, party actualities are to be displayed under the audio column with the name of the person in all caps and what they say in lower caps. Look at the example below.

SYDNEY CROSBY GOES BACK HOME

REPORTER: Luis Almeida

VIDEO	AUDIO
MS TO CU SHOT OF SIDNEY CROSBY, STAR OF THE PITTSBURGH PENGUINS	SFX: SOUND OF HOCKEY GOAL

LS OF MAPLE LEAF FANS SCREAMING "CROSBY!" MS OF PITTSBURGH PENGUINS ARENA, FOLLOWED BY A CU OF PITTSBURGH PENGUIN FANS CONTEMPLATING.	LUIS: It is difficult to believe that start player Sidney Crosby is leaving the Pittsburgh Penguins' franchise.
MS OF REPORTER STEPPING INTO THE PICTURE WITH TORONTO MAPLE LEAF FANS IN THE BACK.	LUIS: His new home is now here in Toronto, Canada and his fans can't wait. Let's listen to what his fans are saying.
CUT TO MALL INT	JOHN: I am so glad Crosby is back.
CU JOHN	He means a lot to us.
CUT RICH	RICH: What a privilege to us here in Canada. I can't believe that Crosby is coming back!
EXT MCU OF LUIS OUTSIDE CANADIAN MALL ADDRESSING CAMERA UNTIL CLOSE.	LUIS: It is hard to believe Sidney Crosby is gone for good. We Pittsburgh Penguin fans will have to accept this fact. From Toronto Canada, this is Luis Almeida from WIUPTV.

REVIEW CHECKLIST

- ✓ All video text is to be in all caps.
- ✓ Reporter voice is to be written in low caps with the name of the reporter in all caps.
- ✓ Party actualities are to be displayed under the audio column with the name of the person in all caps and what they say in lower caps.
- ✓ Camera shots can also be put under the video column in all caps.
- ✓ You should divide the page with video on the left and audio on the right. Both words all caps.

QUESTIONS

1. Explain, in detail, how you would construct a two column feature story.
2. Go online and analyze a two column feature story with a classmate.
3. What are the elements of this form of scriptwriting?
4. Why should a company hire you to write their scripts? Tell me everything you know about this type of scriptwriting.

SAMPLE EXERCISE (Root, Owoc, McClelland, Ranish)

FADE UP FROM BLACK WS CAM 3	**TIFFANY** Hey, there buddy. What are ya doing?
	TYLER Preparing!
	TIFFANY Preparing? For what?
	TYLER Only the best three months of the year!
	TIFFANY Looks a little more like you're preparing to get beat up.
	TYLER There's only one thing that's going to be beating me this summer.
	TIFFANY Should I ask?
	TYLER The ocean, when I'm floating with me, myself, and these three floaties.
	TIFFANY So I take it, you'll be at the beach a lot this summer?
	TYLER You bet your tanning oil I'll be!
	TIFFANY But I don't have any tanning oil.

TYLER That's too bad, Tiff.

TIFFANY Oh yeah? Why?

TYLER Because bronze is beautiful.

TIFFANY You know what's not beautiful—Black and blue!

TYLER Welcome to Indie Rocker's Ball!

CUT TO INTRO   (MUTE MICS)
FADE TO BLACK   FADE UP INTRO MUSIC

FADE FROM BLACK   (UN-MUTE MICS)
WS CAM 3

TIFFANY So, why are you so excited for summer, Tyler?

TYLER I'm not too sure. There's just something about it that gives me a really good feeling inside . . . . It's the same feeling baby teeth give me.

TIFFANY Did you just say baby teeth?

TYLER Yup, baby teeth. There's nothing I'd rather do, than relax with my toes in the fine grains of sand, warm sun shining, and the sounds of baby teeth filling my ears.

TIFFANY Say what? I think you better get that cerebellum of yours examined.

TYLER Why?

TIFFANY Because I'm going to crush it if you don't stop saying ridiculous things like that!

TYLER What, toes?

TIFFANY No! Well, yes, but no. Baby teeth.

TYLER Oh! Baby teeth. They're one of my favorite summertime bands.

TIFFANY That's a band?! You should have clarified that.

TYLER Well, maybe you should read the song list before the show.

TIFFANY Excuse me?

TYLER I mean—I'm going to tell our viewers about this band.

CUT TO CU CAM 1   Baby Teeth are an indie rock band that came out of Chicago in 2004. They originally started out as a trio but later accepted a fourth member as a guitarist in 2007. Baby Teeth have released four albums with Lujo Records since 2005 and their latest album, "White Teeth" was released in March. Unfortunately, Baby Teeth are not currently touring.

CUT TO WS CAM 3   **TIFFANY** You know, Tyler all this talk about the beach and summer reminded me of another song for tonight.

TYLER Oh yeah, who?

TIFFANY Firs.

TYLER Hmm, I don't really follow you, Tiff. Furs usually remind me of the winter time or even fall. Not really the summer (chuckles to self). Good try though.

TIFFANY Not furs with a "U," bean brains! Firs with an "I"!

TYLER I still don't understand how that reminds you of the beach.

TIFFANY Well, if YOU would have read the song list for tonight, you'd know that Firs is a band, and the song we will hear is called "Whale in the Night."

TYLER Ok, that makes a little more sense. Let me guess, it reminds you of a majestic sperm whale bathing under the moonlit sky?

TIFFANY What? No! It reminds me of Japanese whale hunters.

TYLER That's disturbing, Tiff. You know that's illegal, right?

TIFFANY What do you light your lantern with at night? Gold fish blubber? I don't think so.

TYLER Well, I think I'd rather hear about the Firs.

CUT TO CU CAM 2   **TIFFANY** Firs are an indie pop-rock band that started in the later end of 2008. Joey Cook and Sophia Cunningham met in Cincinnati, Ohio and began writing music immediately. After five short months together they released a 5-song, self-titled EP, "I Will Return as a Volcano" with Lujo Records. Their second album, "Man In Space," was released in 2009, also on Lujo Records.

WS CAM 3

TYLER Here's, Baby Teeth with "Hustle Beach."

TIFFANY And Firs with "Whale in the Night."

TYLER After that we will head over to Bri and see what musical knowledge she can fill our brains with.

FADE TO BLACK

(MUTE MICS)

ROLL VIDEOS ON VTR

FADE UP VTR AUDIO

FADE TO BLACK

FADE DOWN VTR AUDIO

FADE UP FROM BLACK

CUT TO MID SHOT OF 1ST ACTUALITY ON INDIE ROCKER'S BALL

ACTUALITY #1: Hey guys, Bri here for this week's music news. Irish indie rock band, Two Door Cinema Club, is currently touring the United States for the rest of May and into the month of June.

BRING UP GRAPHIC OF BRI'S NAME

SFX: GRAPHIC ENTER

FADE OUT GRAPHIC OF BRI'S NAME

SFX: GRAPHIC EXIT

CAMERA SLOWLY ZOOMS IN TO A CLOSE UP

BRI: The band is coming back from a standby year, and the tour is a great way to get back into the music industry. They are signed with Kitsune Music where they released their debut album, "Tourist History" on March 1, 2010. This album won the Choice Music Prize for Irish Album of the Year. Also, in January 2011 Two Door Cinema Club was featured on Late Night with Jimmy Fallon where they performed their song "What You Know." Band members consist of Sam Holliday, Alex Trimble, and Kevin Baird.

CAMERA SLOWLY ZOOMS OUT TO A WIDE SHOT

Well that's all the news for today, be sure to tune in next for more IRB music news.

FADE TO BLACK
FADE UP FROM BLACK
FADE UP AUDIO
WS CAM 3

TIFFANY Wow, that was like 'awesome 101' in fewer than three minutes. Such good knowledge. What did you think, Tyler?

TYLER (Blankly staring forward)

TIFFANY Tyler? Hello? Anyone in there?

TIFFANY HITS TYLERS ARM

TYLER Ouch! What was that for?!

TIFFANY I asked you a question, yah beach bum!

TYLER LOOKS AROUND ROOM

TYLER It's never been so quiet.

TIFFANY What are you talking about?

TYLER LOOKS AT TIFFANY

TYLER Why aren't you speaking?

TIFFANY Is this some kind of joke?

TYLER Tiff! I can't hear anything! What's happening?

TIFFANY Are you serious?! What's wrong?

TYLER Ha! Gotcha, I was just joking around. Awe, come on. Don't be mad, Tiff. It was just a joke. I'm really sorry.

TIFFANY That wasn't nice.

TYLER I was just thinking about our next video, "It's Never Been So Quiet" by Tonight is Glory. It's about this zombie apocalypse and everyone is dead and it's really quiet and . . . Well, I'll just let you watch it. I need to get you talking again. Why don't you tell the viewers about this band, Tiff?

CUT TO CU CAM 2

TIFFANY Tonight is Glory is a screamo band that formed out of El Paso, Texas in 2008. Together they have written and released two albums, including their 2008 "Horizons" and their 2009 "The Vision and Reality." There's currently no information in regards to future tour dates or album releases.

CUT TO WS CAM 3

TYLER Here's Tonight is Glory with their 2009 release of its "Never Been So Quiet."

FADE TO BLACK
SWITCH TO VTR AND
PLAY VIDEO

(**MUTE MICS**)

FADE UP VTR AUDIO

FADE TO BLACK
FADE UP FROM BLACK
FADE UP AUDIO
WS CAM 3

FADE DOWN VTR AUDIO

TIFFANY You know whose voice I like to hear?

TYLER Fred Savage?

TIFFANY What? No. I was going to say mine. What made you think of Fred Savage?

TYLER Well, our classic cut is called "Wonder Years" by Wildchild so I figured that you had Fred Savage on your mind.

TIFFANY When does anyone ever have Fred Savage on their mind other than Fred Savage, himself?

TYLER He did narrate his life.

TIFFANY Now, Wildchild . . . That's a different story. He is da bomb!

TYLER I don't think I've ever heard of him before.

TIFFANY Well, Tyler let me enlighten you.

CUT TO CU CAM 2   Wildchild, also known as Jack Brown, is a rapper that has released two solo albums and is also a member of the hip-hop group, Lootpack. The first of Wildchild's two solo albums is called, "Secondary Protocol" which was released on Stones Throw Records. His second is called "Jack of All Trades," and was released on Fat Beats. Wildchild's music has been featured on shows such as Adult Swim and Full Metal Alchemist.

CUT TO WS CAM 3   **TYLER** Sounds like a pretty boss man. Let's hear it!

TIFFANY Here's Wildchild with his song "Wonder Years."

FADE TO BLACK

(**MUTE MICS**)

FADE UP VTR FOR MUSIC VIDEO
FADE TO BLACK

FADE UP VTR AUDIO

FADE UP FROM BLACK
FADE UP AUDIO
WS CAM 3

FADE DOWN VTR AUDIO

TYLER Well, it's about that time, Tiff.

TIFFANY To say your prayers?

TYLER Or . . . to say goodbye?

FADE MUSIC UP AND UNDER
CAM 3 ZOOM OUT EWS

TIFFANY Fine, if we have to.

TYLER Remember to like us on Facebook.

TIFFANY And to follow us on YouTube.

TYLER And to chirp us on Twitter.

TIFFANY And that there's 82 miles of beaches in Nantucket.

TYLER Really?

FADE UP MUSIC MORE
START CREDITS
FADE MUSIC DOWN
FADE TO BLACK

TIFFANY Adios!

SAMPLE EXERCISE (Barron, Denio, St. Clair)

IUP OFFERS CLASSES BEYOND THE NORM

REPORTERS: Kyra Barron, Alyssa St. Clair, and Quinn Denio

VIDEO	AUDIO
FADE IN TO MS OF KYRA	KYRA: Students in college want to study things that are interesting, and universities are starting to listen to their student body. IUP offers quite a few special topics classes in a variety of majors. Alyssa and Quinn are here to tell you everything you need to know from the students themselves.
FADE OUT; FADE IN TO ALYSSA AND QUINN FULL BODY SHOT	ALYSSA: We are here with IUP student Josh Peters who during spring semester of 2012 took a class called "Zombie Narratives in Literature and Film." Josh, what kind of things did you learn about in this class?
CUT TO JOSH; OVER THE SHOULDER SHOT	JOSH: Zombies, of course! We did a lot of readings about zombie lit and watched a lot of movies in and out of class.
CUT TO ALYSSA; OVER THE SHOULDER SHOT	ALYSSA: What work was required?

CUT TO JOSH; OVER THE SHOULDER SHOT

JOSH: We had to write a response to each of the movies and readings for class. There were a lot of discussions on our opinions which was really cool because we got to hear what everyone thought about the same topics.

CUT TO ALYSSA; OVER THE SHOULDER SHOT

ALYSSA: What was the most interesting discussion topic?

CUT TO JOSH; OVER THE SHOULDER SHOT

JOSH: Well, considering "Zombieland" is one of my favorite movies I would have to say that discussion was pretty interesting. "Zombieland" covers humor, reality, fantasy and basic life lessons all in one movie. It was also really awesome to talk about Zombies in popular culture when the class read *American Zombie Gothic: The Rise and Fall (and Rise) of the Walking Dead in Popular Culture.*

CUT TO ALYSSA; OVER THE SHOULDER SHOT

ALYSSA: Did you discuss any theories about 2012?

CUT TO JOSH; OVER THE SHOULDER SHOT

JOSH: Yeah, we talked about that for a week in class. I would say the majority of the class decided if the world does end it won't be due to zombies. Although, I think secretly after this class we all wish there would be a zombie apocalypse!

CUT TO ALYSSA; OVER THE SHOULDER SHOT

ALYSSA: What was the worst part of the class?

CUT TO JOSH; OVER THE SHOULDER SHOT

JOSH: The class itself was amazing, but there was a lot of reading and writing to do. It makes sense because it's an honors course, but sometimes it was overwhelming. The last assignment made it all worth it though because we got to dress up in our best zombie attire and hang out in the Oak Grove while telling other students some of the things that we had learned. And of course we got food.

CUT TO ALYSSA; OVER THE SHOULDER SHOT

ALYSSA: Would you recommend this class to other students?

CUT TO JOSH; OVER THE SHOULDER SHOT

JOSH: Oh, absolutely! I think that IUP should make it a non-honors course available to all of the students. It is a great experience and it really is a topic I did not expect to study in college. I hope that other students find interest in the subject and give the class a shot if it is offered again.

CUT TO JOSH AND ALYSSA; MS

ALYSSA: Anything else you want to tell your fellow students?

CUT TO JOSH; MS

JOSH: I recommend all zombie readings and movies to everyone. Especially if you are a zombie fanatic and enjoy reading and watching different peoples' opinions and ideas about the way zombies look and act. After this class, I will most likely continue to read zombie novels and watch zombie movies, but now I will be able to do so with background knowledge about the subject.

CUT TO JOSH AND ALYSSA; MS

ALYSSA: Josh, thank you so much for sharing your experience with your fellow student body! Good luck during the zombie apocalypse if it happens.

CUT TO JOSH; MS

JOSH: Thanks for having me! Like *Dawn of the Dead* pointed out, "When there's no more room in hell, the dead will walk the earth."

FADE OUT; FADE IN TO MS OF KYRA

KYRA: So, there you have it. IUP offers a class on zombies! What else are the students studying? Are these special topics useful? We are about to find out more about these unusual classes that students find so interesting. Next, Quinn is going to tell us about another "unusual" course being offered for the Fall Semester of 2012.

FADE IN TO MS OF QUINN

SFX: SHORT CLIP OF HARRY POTTER THEME SONG

MS OF QUINN

QUINN: Hello, everyone. I am very excited to tell you all about the English course, English 430: Major British Authors, which, next semester, will focus on J.K Rowling and her world-famous Harry Potter series! Yes, you heard correctly: there is a Harry Potter class at IUP! Here to give us some more details is the professor . . . or headmistress, Dr. Heather Powers. Dr. Powers, what will this Harry Potter class entail?

CUT TO HEATHER; OVER THE SHOULDER SHOT

HEATHER: Well, this is certainly one course you will not want to miss! In my class, you will get sorted into a house, explore the Wizarding World through critical theory, learn about adaptation theory, analyze popular culture, and complete an independent research project. And don't forget Quidditch!

CUT TO QUINN; MS

QUINN: So basically, this is a class that any Harry Potter fan will be able to appreciate. Are there any prerequisites needed to register for your course?

CUT TO HEATHER; MS

HEATHER: If you have read all of the Harry Potter books, you are qualified to take this course. All other pre-requisites will be waived upon application to the English Department secretary.

CUT TO QUINN; MS

QUINN: Great! That certainly makes it more accessible to non-English majors. Why do you feel that this is an important and beneficial class for students to take?

CUT TO HEATHER; OVER THE SHOULDER SHOT

HEATHER: It will be beneficial because we will learn from the skills which have made the Harry Potter series more than beloved, but truly an absolute obsession among millions. In addition to important themes presented in the series, we will consider what made her writing so magical for so many. Muggle writers will be able to explore these topics and techniques in order to improve their critical thinking skills and even their own writing and style.

CUT TO QUINN; MS

QUINN: What do you think is the most difficult part of this class?

CUT TO HEATHER; MS	HEATHER: Probably the intensive writing and the independent project. It will be somewhat tedious, but definitely worthwhile!
CUT TO QUINN; OVER THE SHOULDER SHOT	QUINN: Anything else you'd like to share with us?
CUT TO HEATHER; OVER THE SHOULDER SHOT	HEATHER: Just that I am very excited for this course next semester and I hope you all are too! So grab your broomsticks, and get ready for an adventure!
CUT TO QUINN AND HEATHER; MS	QUINN: Dr. Powers, thank you so much for talking with us today and we wish you all the best!
CUT TO HEATHER; MS	HEATHER: It was my pleasure. I hope to see you all at Hogwarts next semester!
FADE OUT; FADE IN TO MS OF KYRA	KYRA: Thank you, Quinn and Dr. Powers. So, not only can IUP students learn about zombies, but they can also learn about the magical world of Harry Potter. Are these the only two "unusual" classes that IUP has to offer? Well, as it turns out, there are more! Next, Alyssa will be joining us once again to talk to us about another special topics course that is taking IUP by storm.

ZOOM INTO PICTURE OF LADY GAGA	SFX CLIP FROM "BORN THIS WAY"
FADE IN TO MS OF ALYSSA	ALYSSA: According to the *New York Times,* the University of South Carolina has created a sociology course called "Lady Gaga and the Sociology of Fame." It has been rumored that this course will soon become a part of IUP's sociology courses. The primary goal of this course is to examine the different dimensions of fame through the career of Lady Gaga. Today, I'm here with Anita and Tyler to discuss their thoughts on the possibility of a course similar to this one coming to IUP. First we'll start with Anita. How are you doing today and have you heard about the potential Lady Gaga course coming to IUP?
CUT TO ANITA; MS	ANITA: Hi, thank you for having me. I'm very excited to be here. And yes I actually have heard that rumor floating around and I've been wondering if it's true!
CUT BACK TO ALYSSA; CUT TO OVER THE SHOULDER SHOT	ALYSSA: How would you feel if this course came to IUP?

CUT TO MEDIUM SHOT OF BOTH ANITA AND ALYSSA; CUT TO CLOSE UP OF ANITA

ANITA: I personally am a huge fan of Lady Gaga and I support her 100%, so I would be absolutely thrilled if IUP offered a sociology course on her, especially since I am a sociology major.

MS OF ALYSSA AND ANITA; CUT TO CLOSE UP OF ALYSSA

ALYSSA: I am a huge fan of Lady Gaga as well but with that being said, do you really believe a sociology course on Lady Gaga would be beneficial to students?

CUT TO MS OF ANITA

ANITA: I really do believe that it would be beneficial and I'm not just saying that because I am a huge fan of hers. Lady Gaga has completely changed pop culture, and she is a huge role model for not only the American society, but also the rest of the world. There is a lot we could learn from her and from the dimensions of fame through her career.

CUT TO MS OF ALYSSA

ALYSSA: Very interesting thank you Anita. I am also here with communications major Tyler Rupert, who looks like he is feeling a little different than how Anita feels about this potential Lady Gaga course. What do you think Tyler?

CUT TO CLOSE UP
OF TYLER

TYLER: Personally, I think that course would be slightly ridiculous. I think Lady Gaga is weird, I'm not a fan.

CUT BACK TO MS
OF ALYSSA

ALYSSA: So you wouldn't take this course if it was offered at IUP?

CUT TO TYLER; MS

TYLER: I wouldn't. But at the same time, I can see how this course might be valuable and interesting to a sociology major who is also a big fan of Lady Gaga. Although she is completely strange, she definitely has made an impact on society, and that is always something that is important to learn about.

CUT BACK TO ALYSSA; MS

ALYSSA: Thanks for your thoughts Tyler! And there you have it! A potential course on Lady Gaga is actually seen as valuable to a few students at IUP. It will be interesting to see if this course actually becomes a part of the Sociology department in the very near future! Back to you Kyra!

CUT BACK TO KYRA; MS

KYRA: Wow sounds interesting, thanks Alyssa! Sounds like a lot of exciting things are happening around IUP! Unfortunately, that is all we have time for today. See you next time!

ZOOM OUT TO LONG
SHOT AND FADE TO BLACK

SFX MUSIC

EXERCISE

You are to write a three page two column feature story about a topic of your choice. You must include camera shots, special effects, actualities, a character, locations (such as mall location), as well as a catchy title. Make sure to write at least 7 pages for this project. Have fun!

REFERENCES

Camera Shots. (2011). Retrieved October 21, 2011, from http://www.mediacollege
.com.

Garvey, D., & Rivers, W. (1982). *Broadcast Writing.* Longman, New York, NY.

Hyde, S. (2002). *Ideas to Script: Storytelling for today's media.* Allyn & Bacon, Boston, MA.

Straczynski, J. (1997). *The Complete Book of Scriptwriting.* Synthetic Worlds, Cincinnati, OH.

Stuart, H. (2003). *Idea to Script. Storytelling for Today's Media.* Pearson Publishing, Boston, MA.